Praise for *Busting Your Corporate Idol*

Busting Your Corporate Idol exposes the dangers of organizational commitment taken to extremes. He shares practical advice for balancing career success and living a meaningful and authentic life. If you are losing the joy in your work and your life, this is the book for you.

—Karin Hurt
Executive Director in the telecommunications industry and founder of letsgrowleaders.com

How I wish I had had this book when I was in corporate America — that was the recurring thought as I read Greg Marcus's book. But for each time that thought occurred, it was countered by another: Corporate America or not, it really doesn't matter — the principles within this book will benefit me in ALL of my interactions, from professional relationships to personal ones to my children!

It's clear to me now that I did idolize the company. I realized it when I read the author's words: "There is a line where healthy company loyalty morphs into corporate idolatry." But why I wondered? For me, it was because I allowed the company to become my identity, so in spending more time at work, in giving the company more of ME, my identity grew stronger and I was better able to feel my worth -- as an employee, as a person....

—Leslie Green
Author of Love, Trust and Pixie Dust

Busting your Corporate Idol is a concise and well-written book that is also very timely in describing a common and avoidable malady of our modern era. If you are someone who is allowing work to dominate your time and life, potentially at the cost of your health or relationships, then you absolutely must read this book. Greg offers a perspective that will actually lead you to be MORE EFFECTIVE AT WORK, while allowing you MORE FREE TIME. This is a great paradox of life, and Greg will explain why and how to grasp this important key. I learned the lessons in this book the hard way, and it is now very easy for me to spot people in the workplace that are in the spiral. Please, do yourself a favor - take some time to read this book and you will be rewarded with a new perspective and constructive steps toward optimizing your life balance.

—Arthur P. Review on Amazon.com

"Busting Your Corporate Idol" is chicken soup for the overworked soul, but with an interesting spice thrown into the broth. Greg Marcus frames the harried worker's dilemma in spiritual terms, even challenging readers to consider whether their pattern of giving too much of their lives to the company may represent (at least per the Hebrew Scriptures) the sin of idolatry. Marcus' main thesis will resonate strongly with adherents of the world's great monotheistic religions. For others who suffer from an imbalance of work to the rest of life, there is enough practical advice that can stand independently of the "idolatry" thesis to make this a worthwhile read.

Marcus' intended audience will find many relevant ideas and much encouragement here. He illustrates each major point with at least one story - often based on interviews with people in the biotechnology industry, with which he's most familiar - but the stories are well told, so that whatever industry and level readers are at, the dots that connect to their own situations should be easy to trace.

—Dave Todaro, Review on Amazon.com

"How To Reconnect With Values & Regain Control Of Your Life" is a powerful message for many people, who work exhaustive overtimes in their skyscrapers. There are quite a number of aspects in the Greg Marcus' writing that I enjoyed.

—Leo Ostapiv, Review on Amazon.com
Author of Home Finance For Couples

Greg Marcus does not suffer fools lightly when he exposes the concept of corporate idolatry in Busting Your Corporate Idol. He uncovers what keeps many people up at night. Idolization can creep up on you and take over before you comprehend it. The good news is that his book opens up our hearts and our minds to the realities and possibilities of the workplace. He tells the story of work like it is or may be and gives us tools to understand how to make our work and our life better. If something in this book makes you a bit uneasy; use that to find your balance. It reminded me that we can actually pursue the definition of work as expressed in The Prophet by Kahlil Gibran... "Work is love made visible".

—Patricia J. Kempthorne
Founder & Executive Director, Twiga Foundation

Greg's story and his book reflect his revelations in an extremely personal and gripping way that forces you to think about your own priorities and how they fit into a work/life balance. It's the beginning of the journey toward taking control of your situation and making certain that you are there for the people around who need you, including yourself. Greg's writing is modern, genuine and thoughtful. It will help move life forward.

—Rick R. Amazon.com review

Busting Your Corporate Idol may seem like heresy to the hard charging, work sixteen hours-a-day MBA crowd, but Dr. Marcus is on to something. Just like the pioneers into green business, sustainability, Corporate Social Responsibility (CSR) and business ethics, Dr. Marcus boldly throws the gauntlet down for all of us to rethink our personal bottom lines so that we may challenge our blind allegiances to the corporation and instead foster a deeper sense of what it means to have a life that's in balance.

—Jarie Bolander,
From review on The Daily MBA.Com

Marcus' book isn't meant to accelerate readers' careers but to put their careers in proper perspective. ... it's designed to be imminently practical; chapters dispense actionable advice on "The Secret to Leaving Early," "Creating Rituals for a People-First Life" and "How You Can Kick the Habit of Overwork." Chapters conclude with a worksheet with discussion questions and helpful tips.

—Kirkus Reviews

Greg's book serves as a clear and concise reminder that what is "best for the company" is not necessarily "what is best." Reflecting on his own path away from the false gods of corporate obedience, he maps out strategies for regaining control of our priorities – lessons that will prove useful in any organizational arena.

—D. A. Wolf
Writer, independent marketing and social media consultant, and founder of Dailyplateofcrazy.com

Greg's writing and positive messaging gave me just that added boost to feel good about my decision to resign from my last position. Work/family balance was suffering and the stress wasn't worth it. I then spent part of the summer traveling the country with my children. We have special memories that will be with us for a lifetime. I found a new gig at the end of the summer, and I plan to be more disciplined from the get go about setting boundaries and sticking to them. It will make me happier at home and more effective at work.

—Maggie Rougier-Chapman, sales and marketing professional

BUSTING YOUR CORPORATE IDOL

SELF-HELP FOR THE CHRONICALLY OVERWORKED

GREG MARCUS, Ph.D.

Idolbuster Coaching Institute
San Carlos, California

Busting Your Corporate Idol: Self-Help for the Chronically Overworked
Author: Greg Marcus, Ph.D.
Development Editor: Hillel Black
Copy Editor: Laura Carlson
Print Layout by Jake Muelle
Cover Design by Ranilo Cabo (line 14) via 99designs.com
Internal Image Design by Monika Zec via 99designs.com

Copyright © 2013-2014 by Greg Marcus
All rights reserved. No part of this book may be reproduced in any form by any means without the expressed permission of the author. This includes reprints, excerpts, photocopying, recording, or any future means of reproducing text. If you would like to do any of the above, please seek permission from the Idolbuster Coaching Institute at idolbuster.com.
First print edition 2014

Published in the United States by the Idolbuster Coaching Institute.
ISBN 978-0-9899158-1-6

For information about bulk discounts, please email The Idolbuster Coaching Institute at info@idolbuster.com

Note From the Author
Busting Your Corporate Idol: Self-Help for the Chronically Overworked is a book full of stories. Each chapter begins with a story from my life. And many chapters include stories from the thirty men and women I interviewed for the book. Most were directors and vice presidents from mid-size to large corporations. Each story provides a snapshot of the corporate life, together crafting a mosaic from a broad range of age, experience, and industries. Stories were shared in confidence, and unless otherwise noted have been camouflaged to communicate the humanity while maintaining confidentiality. This book previously was published with the subtitle "How To Reconnect With Values & Regain Control Of Your Life."

To Rachel, Hannah, and Becky—the real stars of my life

Contents

Part 1: Corporate Idolatry Busted............................1

    CHAPTER 1   My Corporate Idolatry................3
    CHAPTER 2   Why Idolatry?......................15
    CHAPTER 3   The Corporation—
                        The *Real* American Idol..............31

Part 2: Living With Corporate Idolatry......................55

    CHAPTER 4   Who To Trust—the Scorpion,
                        the Fox, or the Wolf?................57
    CHAPTER 5   The Pivotal Role of Circumstance—
                        Hot Tables and Bad Breaks............77
    CHAPTER 6   Corporate Culture and the
                        Invisible Hand of the Company 95

Part 3: The Post-Idolatry Life 107

    CHAPTER 7   Secure Your Identity................109
    CHAPTER 8   Build Your Community 127
    CHAPTER 9   Paint Your Environment.............145
    CHAPTER 10   The Balanced Life 171

Notes...187

Acknowledgements.....................................197

PART 1
Corporate Idolatry Busted

CHAPTER 1
My Corporate Idolatry

*M*y hectic life had become a whirlwind, my days and weeks a blur. I didn't have time to stop, relax, and think ahead. Life felt out of control, a roller coaster that oscillated between screaming drops and anxiety-ridden climbs. Looking back, I was at the mercy of forces beyond my control—layoffs and reorganizations—and I was expected to do what my boss asked of me, whether it was reasonable or not. Further, I was expected to do what is best for the company, even if it was not in the best interests of the customers, my coworkers, or myself. I was told that the same problems exist in every company, implying that I could change my address, but it wouldn't change my life. When I was caught up in this vortex, it was hard to look ahead to a time when I wouldn't be experiencing the same thing. I am not the only one who feels this way. An executive job coach who works in Silicon Valley told me the number one question he gets is "How do I get my life back?"

The answer for me came in an unexpected place and at an unexpected time. I had gone twenty hours without food or water, and suddenly discovered that my life had been out to lunch. It was Yom Kippur, the Jewish Day of Atonement, and I was nearing the end of the traditional sundown-to-sundown fast. The more spiritual among us might say that God spoke to me in that moment. It didn't feel like that to me, but my mind did open and a new idea took root. It changed my life.

No one is more surprised than me that I am writing a book inspired by religious teachings. I was raised in a mostly secular

Jewish household, where we attended services only twice a year for the major holidays. I was a scientist for ten years, getting a Ph.D. from MIT in Molecular Biology and conducting my post-doctoral work at Stanford.[1] For the next ten years I worked in marketing. My scientist friends teased me for going over to the dark side. It was more true than they realized, but I loved it. To this day, I cannot believe how much I enjoyed writing ad copy. Life is full of surprises, and on Yom Kippur I got a huge surprise that changed my life.

I take Yom Kippur, the Day of Atonement, seriously every year. It is the day when Jews around the world take a day off from work, don't eat or drink, go to services, and well, atone. I look forward to the chance to reflect on my life, to think about what I've done wrong, and to make amends. While prayer is sufficient for "sins against God," prayer alone does not suffice for sins against other people. We must apologize, make right the wrong if we can, and resolve to behave differently in the future if a similar situation arises.

One year, I called a coworker somewhat sheepishly at three in the afternoon to apologize for a practical joke that had gotten out of hand six months earlier. I felt better afterwards. Another year I realized that the Jews invented the day off. Prior to Shabbat, aka the Sabbath, we were expected to work every day. I later learned that the Greeks and Romans used to lampoon the Jews about Shabbat, calling the weekly high holiday a waste of time. The purpose of rest was to prepare for more work, while leisure was something reserved for the wealthy. To be honest, I was not then or now particularly good at taking a day off.

But my insight about the day off inspired me to pay greater attention to the words of the prayers the following Yom Kippur, and in 2005 I made a discovery that truly changed my life. I was sitting alone with my thoughts in the Flint Center, an old-school performing arts auditorium in Cupertino, California, big enough to fit my entire Reform Jewish congregation of 2,500 members. It was late in the day, and I was feeling tired and a bit woozy. It is my favorite time, as my mind sometimes goes to new places.

That afternoon, I noticed how often the prayers made reference to one God, and I wondered about the sin of idolatry. I started to dismiss idolatry as an archaic idea, no longer relevant in the modern world, when I remembered a phrase I had heard many times from my bosses and colleagues: "You need to do what is best for the company." I was suddenly uncomfortable.

The moment lasted a long time. Idolatry is the worship of a statue or a false god. I don't worship statues or … I remembered my company's brand logo. That symbol was displayed in practically every room of every building of the company, including the branches in Europe, Asia, and South America. It was on every piece of paper. It was on some of my favorite clothes. Trying to reassure myself, I thought about the nature of a corporation. It didn't help. A corporation is an artificial person as recognized by the Supreme Court of the United States. It's a formless and shapeless entity. There are a lot of them, and they have different cultures and values.

I thought about the time I was scolded for an innocuous suggestion to embed the brand symbol as part of a cool graphic in a marketing piece. It kind of puzzled me at the time. *What's the big deal?* But it was a big deal, like an unwritten commandment. THOU SHALL NOT MESS WITH THE BRAND SYMBOL.

The company is like an idol, and when we do "what is best for the company," instead of "what is best," we are offering blind obedience. I also realized that we only used that phrase to justify something unpleasant, like a canceled project, a layoff, or shipping a product that wasn't ready to go, knowing the customers were going to be mad.

All of these thoughts took less than a second. I describe it sequentially, but it all arrived at the same time. There was more.

I thought about the sacrifices I had made for the company, such as my fitness, my sleep, my time with family, and my focus. In fact, the company gave out an award at the quarterly "All Hands Meeting" employee meeting to the person who showed the most company spirit. This company spirit often came in the form of getting on a plane at a moment's notice, or canceling a vacation. Every quarter I was disappointed that I didn't get it.

My corporation was my idol. I knew it was true in the pit of my stomach, but my brain wanted more information about idolatry. A few days later I found an article on the Internet called, "What is So Terrible About Idolatry?" by Rabbi Tzvi Freeman, editor of "Ask the Rabbi" at Chabad.org. Rabbi Freeman described what is distinctive about pagan idolatry. "If you don't like what one god demands of you, you go find another god more to your taste. … After all, none of them is supreme, none is all-powerful."

The numerous gods are similar to the corporate world. There are many different companies, each with its own culture and values. And if you don't like the values of your company, you can move to another. For example, if you think your company is not honest enough with customers, you can find one that is more transparent. But if you think transparency is bad for business, there is a company for you too. There is no overriding set of values held by all companies, beyond the need to be profitable.

I had been a true believer in my company. I thought the company had a mission to change the world, and I needed to devote myself to help the company achieve these laudable goals. I thought I was getting paid a lot of money to change the world. In reality, the company's first, second, and third priorities were to make money. Some very good things did come from the company—we developed cutting edge tools for scientific research that led to thousands of papers in the top journals. However, the price I paid in terms of my health and happiness was very high. I was literally killing myself for the company.

At that time, the most important thing in my life was the company. I am ashamed to admit it, but it was true. I had always told myself that my wife and children were the top priority, but when I look at my actions, decisions, and time spent, it was all about the company. I thought about work in the shower. I talked on my cell phone as I drove in to work, and as I drove home at night. I worked after dinner, and I had trouble falling asleep because I was going over the day in my head. The next day I would get up at five AM to work on email and to call my colleagues in Europe. I worked on most weekend days. The more I sacrificed, the more important the company became to me, which in turn led to more sacrifices.

My insight on Yom Kippur set off a chain of dominos. Once I saw the world in this new way, there was no going back. In the past, I had unsuccessfully tried to change my priorities. This time I went a step further and changed my values. My family and my health *had* to come before the company. Lo and behold the priorities in my life changed. It didn't happen overnight, but over time small incremental changes made a big difference. Even when I was working close to one hundred hours a week, I always ate breakfast and dinner with my family. It was a line in the sand, a boundary I never crossed, and doing so served as a model for the additional changes to come.

I made a conscious choice to work fewer hours. Instead of thinking in a negative way, beating myself up to work less, I focused on the positive.

My health is important. I need to stop working by 9:30 PM, so I have time to wind down and get to sleep.

Then it became *I need to stop working by 9:00 PM, so my wife and I can spend some time together.*

Although I didn't realize it at the time, choosing an action that reinforces a value is a virtuous cycle because the action itself reinforces the value, making it easier to take a similar action the next time. I will discuss this at greater length later in the book.

During the year I transitioned from working ninety to less than sixty hours per week. I started learning more about the teachings of Judaism. My wife and I elected not to send our kids to Sunday school for religious education. I hated Sunday school as a kid. It was boring, irrelevant, and seemed like an onerous, guilt-driven obligation. Instead, we enrolled in a family-based education program, which had sessions of family learning time, followed by separate adult and age-appropriate kid learning. These sessions included snack. Every week the adults gathered for wine, humus, and chocolate cookies. It helped us get to know the other families.

My fascination with idolatry grew. As I learned more about it, I found more connections to my corporate life and surprising solutions in ancient texts. For example, according to the twelfth century Rabbi Maimonides' *Laws of Idolatry*, it is forbidden to wear the clothes of idolators. Maimonides reasoned that wearing the clothes of idol-worshippers was a way of giving tacit approval to the idolator's value system and made it more likely that the wearer would adhere to it. On a lark, I stopped wearing company T-shirts on weekends, and found it helped me keep my mind off of work.

I wrote a short essay on Corporate Idolatry and handed it out in a one-hour discussion section the following Yom Kippur. The turnout was high for one of these groups, about twenty people, and the debate was fierce. My thesis was simple: when we do what is "best for the company," instead of "what is best," we are practicing a form of idolatry.

One man in his late fifties objected in a soft-spoken, kindly way. "I've been in the corporate world a long time. Sometimes things go astray, but as long as you do what is best for the customer, you will be fine."

I wasn't sure what to say when a woman piped up from across the room. "But what about the workers? My husband was told that if he didn't push his group to work every weekend in order to make the timeline, he would be out of a job. The customers will be fine, but the employees are being driven to exhaustion. We aren't twenty-something kids anymore. His company is hardly a start up, but that is the type of time and commitment they expect from everyone. Treating people that way goes against his values, but he needs the job and feels like he is between a rock and a hard place."

The discussion was passionate; the pain was real and prevalent. My ideas had led people to think about their relationship with the employer differently. I felt encouraged to stick with the changes I was making in my life.

Change is often painful, and this was no exception. Doing my part to help other people and to help the group was important to me. I wondered if I was being selfish by doing less at times for the company. Messages at work about being a team player reinforced this notion. Doing less for the company meant doing less for the people on my team. Somehow, it didn't seem right, until I came across the following passage written more than 2,000 years ago by Rabbi Hillel: "If I am not for myself, who will be for me? If I am only for myself, what am I? If not now, when?"

This was like a lightning bolt—of course I have a right to take care of myself. When I cut back on my devotion to the company, it gave me space to allow many positive things to happen. My life got better.

And I was mentally prepared when I was laid off a year later. If I had still been caught up in the company, I would have been devastated. But I was exhilarated, and my wife was thrilled. I packed up my stuff, said a few goodbyes, and drove up the Central Expressway to the Peninsula Creamery, where I had a burger medium rare and a milkshake with coffee ice cream and hot fudge.

The next two months were great, a paid vacation. I went to the gym every morning, came home for lunch, took a nap, watched *Star Trek*, and cooked dinner. Not only was my blood pressure down, but life was also much less stressful, which was also good for my wife and kids.

When I started my next job (after my two month "paid vacation"), I worked hard to avoid identifying myself with the company. I was a professional. My work was high quality but transactional and no longer a mission. I didn't mind that I wasn't working on the most cutting-edge, high profile project because I could see the price people on that team were paying. Also, I consciously put some of my energy into building a community for myself with people outside of my workplace.

So in 2009, when I found myself unhappy at this next job, I was able to walk away. I didn't like the company, some of the people, or the product I was managing. I needed to do something different, and that was never going to happen as long as I was in that job.

My wife and I talked about my resignation for two months before I pulled the trigger. Even with my reduced hours, having two young kids and two high-powered careers made it crazy at home. Things were fine, unless something unexpected came up, like a broken car or a sick kid. And it felt like something came up almost every week.

My two-month paid vacation a few years earlier showed us how much easier life could be. We looked at the budget and figured out how long we could support our family on just her salary. We've gone much longer than we originally estimated because we don't spend as much on stuff. I think I bought stuff as a palliative for stress.

Leaving my job allowed me to see things I was not aware of. One afternoon, I walked past the door of the living room and stopped to watch my six year old daughter play with a friend. They were sitting on the floor cross-legged, talking quietly to each other. I couldn't hear what they were saying, but they were so intense and serious. I had seen them play before, but it was always rambunctious and wild. If I hadn't been home, I would have missed this ordinary but irreplaceable moment.

My life was better. Much better.

I rediscovered the great joys that I hadn't even noticed where missing. I now enjoyed my meals instead of pounding them down or eating mechanically while my mind whirled around my unending workday. I was well rested and found that sex was even better when I wasn't stressed. And because I wasn't stressed, I could be there, in the moment, for my wife and kids. They became less stressed too.

A few months after I left the corporate world, two former colleagues independently told me that I looked ten years younger. Frankly, I was shocked to hear that. Being in my early forties didn't bother me, but if I had recently looked like I was in my fifties, that was disturbing, dismaying, horrifying. I never thought of myself as one of those people who was prematurely aged by the hardship of the job. But I was. *Best not to dwell on it. Be thankful it is behind you, and make sure you don't end up there again.*

I heard something else from former colleagues, especially the men. "I'm jealous. I wish I could do what you did and spend more time with my kids." A few people told me they were inspired to make a change.

Life is like an eleven-sided triangle. You can look at life from a lot of different directions, and see many different triangles. All of them are correct, but none of them are complete. *Busting Your Corporate Idol* presents another lens with which to examine the world, a lens that helped me see why my life was out of control and what needed to change to make it right. Reconnecting with my values was like getting a GPS for my life—I could now drive to a better place, one street at a time.

Would you like to feel empowered to set different priorities and make different choices in your life? Would you like the option to remain employed in the corporate world, but with a better awareness of your true values? By the end of the book you'll have stories that inspire you and a basket of recipes to help you change.

So pick up your hammer, and let's get to work.

Chapter 1 Questions & Tips

Take a few moments to inventory your life. Begin by closing your eyes and breathing deeply to clear your mind. Now, think about the following:

1. What is most important to you? Is it your health, your family, your friends? Is it your company, your career, your status, your income? Is it a cause to change the world in some way?

2. Now think about how you spend your time. How many hours of sleep do you get? What time do you go to bed and get up in the morning? How many hours a day do you work? How often do you check email, respond to text messages, or take phone calls after hours? If you were to get a phone call from work while on a date, would you answer it? (Not should, would.)

3. Based on your answers to #2, what is most important to you? What value system is guiding your life?

CHAPTER 2

Why Idolatry?

I did not get my first real job until I was over thirty, thanks to the ten years I spent in the academic world as a scientist in graduate school and as a postdoctoral fellow. My twenties were spent in the lab, and I loved it. Well, I should be careful how I say that – lab work at the bench was a grind, often frustrating and repetitive. I loved thinking up experiments, interpreting the data, and the rush I felt when something was working. After three years, I got my first breakthrough result at about ten o'clock at night. I rushed around the floor looking for other people to share it with – I found plenty.

The following weekend I attended a party, and I remember going on and on to a female classmate about the very long hours I was working, how well things were going, and how happy I was. Two years later, we started dating after running into each other at another party. This time, I paid attention to her and didn't talk about work. We've been married fifteen years.

My issues with overwork started early in my adult life. For many years, I had a sense of mission about my work. Still, you'd think a twenty-something guy would have his priorities straight when at a party talking to a pretty woman. Yes, she was also a scientist, but to brag about how many hours I was working was a harbinger of things to come. It certainly didn't seem like idolatry. I was just following my passions, and doing what I thought it took to get the job done.

Perhaps you are or you know someone who is "all in" when it comes to the company. I interviewed "George," a former IT manager in the financial industry, who described a payroll manager he used to work with. "[The manager] had two young girls, but he thrilled to the fact that the CFO of the company could call him Thursday night at nine o'clock and he would be there to pick up the phone. That thrilled him. He seemed to have Bigibank through his veins. Little to no quality time with his kids."

Mr. Bigiblood made the company a higher priority than his family on a day-to-day basis. Not only did he take after hours phone calls, it "thrilled him." There are legitimate circumstances when it is necessary to take an after hours call. But when the call becomes a source of pride and boasting, I see a red flag, warning that values and priorities are out of kilter. I'm sure that Mr. Bigiblood loved his kids, but in the moment his work was a higher priority than his family.

When I was working all the time, I never second-guessed my commitment to the company, even when I was making decisions that I regret today. Not only did I drink the Kool-Aid, I served it. I bought into the idea that we needed to do what was best for the company, and everything else came later. It wasn't conscious, but on a day-to-day basis, I made choices that increased my work hours at the expense of my home and health. Throughout the book, I will refer to this as a company-first value system.

Values are the morals that define and set the boundaries for our behavior. They are the line we won't cross, what we will go out of our way to do, and what we will pretend that we didn't see. Sometimes company values are defined as a written set of guidelines provided by the company. These often have little bearing on how people act day to day, and therefore aren't really values. Values are something internal, that drive our priorities and decisions.

At some point, everyone does something they are not comfortable with because the company asks them to. The question is whether this happens on a regular basis. And if we follow through on the request the first time, chances are that we won't hesitate to comply the second time. Do you blindly obey the company? Do you internalize company values, aka drink the Kool-Aid? These latter cases constitute idolatry.

Why Idolatry?

Idolatry was the practice of worshipping many different gods (as statues), as opposed to monotheism, the worship on one God. The relevance of idolatry in today's world goes beyond this religious context. Idolatry is about values and standards of behavior that change with circumstances. Monotheism set a single standard of values that are always true, even when we don't follow them. Many idols of the ancient world demanded human sacrifice; monotheism forbade human sacrifice, and taught that every human life was precious.

In his article "What is So Terrible About Idolatry," Rabbi Tzvi Freedman describes idolatry as a system in which people get to choose which rules to follow, because if they didn't like the demands and rules of one god, they could choose to follow another.

To bring this concept into the modern world, imagine that a misfortune strikes your company, for example there is a performance issue with the key product. What does your company ask you to do? Should you be honest and transparent with the customers, or should you spin and cover up the real issue? The "right" thing to do will depend on the values of your company.

Since company A's value system is different from company B's value system, if you allow the company to decide what you should do, you are in effect adopting a changing value system. The alternative is a moral compass that is independent of your company, a set of unchanging values. So if we want to avoid idolatry, what unchanging values should we embrace? My suggestion is to adopt people-first values.

People-First Values

In 1993, 300 representatives of the world's religions met in Chicago in an attempt to define a set of universal ethical principles. They agreed that the Golden Rule is the "key reference point" of a global ethic, because it is found in so many different religions around the world. Table 2.1 has fourteen versions of the Golden Rule from around the world.

While the language is different, I am convinced that these versions of the Golden Rule are all expressing the same core idea: consider the needs of other people *before you take an action*. Put yourself in their shoes. Think how other people will be impacted by your action. Other words that describe the Golden Rule are compassion and empathy. If we understand the impact on others, we are less likely to do something that is hurtful.

Why does this same idea keep showing up independently all over the world? It may be innate. Babies as young as six months seem to have an innate sense of fairness, and prefer puppets who share with other puppets over puppets who did not.[3] Yale professor Paul Bloom, discusses his results:

These findings constitute evidence that preverbal infants assess individuals on the basis of their behavior towards others. This capacity may serve as the foundation for moral thought and action, and its early developmental emergence supports the view that social evaluation is a biological adaptation.[4]

Religion	Statement
Old Testament	Love thy neighbor as thyself Leviticus 19:18[39]
Judaism	That which is hateful to you, do not do to your fellow. That is the whole Torah; the rest is the explanation. Talmud
Christianity	Do to others as you would have them do to you. Luke 6:31
Buddhism	Hurt not others in ways that you yourself would find hurtful. Udana-Varga 5,1
Islam	No one of you is a believer until he desires for his brother that which he desires for himself. Sunnah
Hinduism	This is the sum of duty; do naught onto others what you would not have them do unto you. Mahabharata 5:1517
Confucianism	Never impose on others what you would not choose for yourself. Analects 12:2
Jainism	Just as pain is not agreeable to you, it is so with others. Knowing this principle of equality, treat the other with compassion.
Taoism	Regard your neighbor's gain as your gain, and your neighbor's loss as your own loss.
Humanism	Ethic of reciprocity: people should aim to treat each other as they would like to be treated themselves—with tolerance, consideration, and compassion.
Pima Indians (Arizona)	Do not wrong or hate your neighbor. For it is not he who you wrong but yourself.
The Yoruba people of Nigeria	One going to take a pointed stick to pinch a baby bird should first try it on himself to feel how it hurts.
The Ba-Congo people of Angola	O Man, O woman, what you do not like, do not do to your fellows.
The Platinum Rule	Treat others the way they want to be treated.

Table 2.1. Fourteen versions of the Golden Rule from cultures around the world.

In addition, numerous psychology studies have shown that strong connections with other people, especially family and community, are a key to being happy.[5]

In summary, the Golden Rule, because it is found in numerous cultures and religions worldwide, seems to be built on an innate human ability to assess how individuals treat one another. Because the Golden Rule is so widely accepted, and because people were treated so badly in idol-worshipping cultures (think human sacrifice in Mesopotamia, and gladiator combat in Rome), I've realized that the way we should act to avoid idolatry is to follow the Golden Rule.

However, the Golden Rule by itself is not sufficient. While the Golden Rule is in cultures from all over the world, it is not universally practiced within those cultures. Some people are just out for themselves.

Rule of Self-Preservation

Not everyone follows the Golden Rule, which may be a surprise to those who do. For example, "Simon," a director at a mid-sized corporation in the Midwest, was astounded when he discovered that some people don't think like him.

"I was at a management offsite, a touchy feely thing. I brought up the Golden Rule [as a model for how to interact with others]. One guy said, 'That doesn't work for me because I don't care how I am treated.' He was almost sociopathic about it. He would do what it took to get ahead. It wasn't like he was even trying to hide it. That just amazed me that there were people out there like that." Simon discovered that he had been operating according to a different set of values than some of his coworkers, who didn't care how they were treated, and therefore didn't care how they treated other people. Could the person Simon was referring to actually have been a sociopath?

A sociopath is someone who does not have a conscience, and according to Dr. Martha Stout, author of *The Sociopath Next Door*, up to four percent of the population could fit the clinical definition of a sociopath.[6] There is also evidence that the percentage of sociopaths who work in corporations may be significantly higher than the general population.[7] And treating a sociopath "as you would like to be treated" is a recipe to be taken advantage of at best, and inviting disaster at worst.

Okay, maybe talking about sociopaths is a bit extreme, but I am trying to illustrate a point: while The Golden Rule is a universal value, it is not sufficient to cover every circumstance. If we were to implement a Golden Rule life strategy, we would be at a significant disadvantage to people who don't have a conscience. So I have another rule I live by; I call it the Rule of Self-Preservation. Simply put, you have a duty to look out for your own welfare, because if you don't, who will? See Table 2.2.

Rabbi Hillel, who formulated the Jewish version of the Golden Rule, also taught: "If I am not for myself, who will be for me? If I am only for myself, what am I? If not now, when?" Hillel was teaching that we need to both look out for the needs of others, and look out for the needs of ourselves. Many good-hearted people believe that if they do a good job and are helpful to others, they will eventually be recognized and treated fairly. Unfortunately, this is not the case.

Throughout the book, when I refer to people-first values, I mean the Golden Rule and the Rule of Self Preservation. Help others, but don't be a doormat. When I think back on my experience going from working ninety to less than sixty hours a week, following the Golden Rule was responsible for part of the change, but not all of it. For example, my decision to get more sleep and to start exercising regularly were motivated by a desire to help myself, not to help other people.

Quote	Source
Natural law includes our right to self-preservation and forbids humans from taking actions destructive to their own lives.	Thomas Hobbes' Leviathan
We hold these truths to be self-evident, that all men are created equal, that they are endowed by their Creator with certain unalienable Rights, that among these are Life, Liberty and the pursuit of Happiness.	Declaration of Independence
Chi pensa per se, pensa per tre. (Anyone who thinks for himself thinks for three.)	Italian proverb
Put on your [oxygen] mask before assisting others.	Airline safety instruction
If someone has a gun and is trying to kill you, it would be reasonable to shoot back with your own gun. Not at the head, where a fatal wound might result. But at some other body part, such as a leg.	The Dali Lama, answering a question about self defense.
"Pray for what you want, but work for the things you need."	Essential Sufism
Keep five yards from a carriage, ten yards from a horse, and a hundred yards from an elephant; but the distance one should keep from a wicked man cannot be measured.	Indian Proverb
Before all else, be armed.	Niccolo Machiavelli

Table 2.2. Quotes That Support the Rule of Self-Preservation.[8][9][10]

The need to improve his health was also part of George's decision to leave Bigibank. He told me in a quiet voice "I was to the point, and my wife saw it, where it wasn't healthy, physically or spiritually [for me to work at that company]. I was getting short tempered with the family. It wasn't a matter of if [my leaving] should happen; it had to happen."

Idolatry, Penn State's Shame

The 2011 sexual abuse scandal at Penn State University represents a sobering and upsetting example of what can happen when people fall into corporate idolatry. For over forty years Joe Paterno was the football coach at Penn State, and was widely respected as a leader, teacher, and philanthropist. How is it that Paterno and the top officials at Penn State University did not report assistant football coach Jerry Sandusky to the police for child abuse after Sandusky was discovered allegedly sodomizing a boy in the locker room shower? One explanation is corporate idolatry—Penn State University propagated a culture that put the interests of the institution (its football program in particular) ahead of the welfare of people. The high level of news coverage and detailed written reports allow insights into how corporate idolatry impacted people at all levels of the university.

In both 1998 and 2001, Paterno and the top officials at Penn State University did not report assistant football coach Jerry Sandusky to the police for child abuse. In 2012 Sandusky was convicted of forty-five counts that ranged from "endangering the welfare of children" to "involuntary deviate sexual intercourse." Some of these crimes happened after 2001, and would have been prevented if Paterno, and other university officials had informed the police.

According to the report by former FBI Director Louis Freeh, Penn State had a "reverence for football program ingrained at all levels of the university."[11] This started from the top, with a "president who discouraged discussion and dissent," and included the attendant who switched off CNN on the TV in the Penn State student center just before the Freeh Report was released.[12]

Figure 2.1. It was common for graduating students to have their pictures taken with the Nittney Lion (the school mascot), and the giant statue of Joe Paterno. It is almost as if Joe Paterno was as important to the students as the rest of college combined. Ten days after the Freeh report was released, Penn State removed the statue of Joe Paterno.[13]

Why People at Penn State Fell into Idolatry

Penn State University has a culture of idolatry because the culture prioritized football over the safety of children. Does this mean that everyone associated with the university are a bunch of evil idolators? Not at all. But, everyone at PSU is impacted by the pervasive football-first value system. And, people who opposed the football-first value system paid a price. For example, former VP of Student Affairs Vicky Triponey "butted heads with Paterno and his football supporters,"[14] and according to The Daily Beast, was fired for investigating players for allegedly sexual assaults. Triponey's boss, former PSU president Graham Spanier, allegedly gave her poor performance reviews because she "wasn't fitting in with the 'Penn State way.'"[15]

Because the Freeh report, was based on interviews with hundreds of people, we have a unique opportunity to understand why people participated in Penn State's football-first value system. I have seen these same four causes of idolatry in the stories I heard from the corporate world, as well as in the literature that discusses idolatry in the ancient world.

1. **For personal advantage.** I think many of the university officers embraced the culture of idolatry because it gave them perks, power, and wealth. According to the Freeh Report, these men "exhibited a striking lack of empathy for Sandusky's victims by failing to inquire as to their safety and well-being."[16] They were more concerned with the reputation of the institution, and by extension their own reputations. I suspect that Paterno and the others used rationaliza-

tions to ease their consciences, and saw themselves as doing the right thing.

2. **Out of habit and blind obedience.** Timothy Curley, the former athletic director, is described as "a State College native with a long family history at Penn State." Some at PSU referred to Curley as "Paterno's errand boy," and others characterized him as "loyal to a fault to university management and the chain of command; someone who followed instruction regardless of the consequences."[17]

3. **Out of fear.** In the fall of 2000, a janitor saw Sandusky with a boy in the shower. By all accounts, the janitor was devastated by what he had seen but was afraid he would lose his job if he spoke up. He said the following to investigators, "I know Paterno has so much power, [and] if he wanted to get rid of someone, I would have been gone ... football runs this university, and the university would have closed ranks to protect the football program at all costs."[18]

4. **By error.** On November 9, 2011, Joe Paterno was fired from Penn State, and thousands of students rioted, chanting, "One more game." This is what philosophers call "Idolatry by Error." Idolatry by error is a behavior that persists due to cultural traditions whose foundation is based on incorrect information. These kids were raised on the notion that Paterno was a great leader who taught his players how to be great men. In other words, the protesters thought that Paterno had been scapegoated and that they were standing up against a great injustice.

These same four reasons: personal advantage, habit, fear, and error help explain why people practice idolatry throughout the corporate world.

Ten Signs of Corporate Idolatry

For many people, including myself, it is hard to be objective about ourselves, especially when we are in the middle of a situation. If you are wondering if you are someone you know is caught up in corporate idolatry, here are a few warning signs that I gathered from my interviews.

1. You find yourself doing "what is best for the company" instead of "what is best." What's best for the company is not necessarily best for people, including customers, employees, or the public.
2. You joke that you are "married to the company."
3. You are getting persistent feedback from a loved one that you are working too many hours.
4. You are experiencing stress-related illnesses – insomnia, headaches, fatigue, high blood pressure, weight gain. Taking a company-first attitude means that personal health comes second or later.
5. You work more than sixty hours per week.
6. You don't care how you treat people at work as long as the job gets done.
7. You are considered "successful" in your career, but often feel unfulfilled in a way that you cannot define. To go new age for a moment, this is your spiri-

tual side talking to you. Lasting happiness comes through connections to other people, and for some, a spiritual connection to something larger than themselves.

8. Someone says that you are "drinking the Kool-Aid." This phrase comes from the Jonestown Massacre, when people committed ritual suicide at the behest of their cult leader.

9. Your boss skips key political meetings, asking if you can handle them on your own. The boss may be setting you up to take the fall, and blind obedience without political savvy violates the Rule of Self Preservation. See Chapter 4 for more.

10. Feeling indispensible to the company and above politics. From the interviews I conducted, people caught up in a company-first attitude often felt that the company depended on them, which served as a rationalization for working longer hours and sacrificing family and personal time.

Idolatry in a Nutshell

Corporate idolatry is a lifestyle that puts the company first, and therefore makes people a lower priority. No one can put people first all the time, and sometimes we make mistakes. But are these mistakes things that happen once in a while, or are they happening on a daily and weekly basis? By analogy, getting an occasional parking ticket does not make you a parking scofflaw. When it comes to priorities, which comes first, people or the company? Before you answer, think about how you actually spend your time.

Think about the decisions you make when you have a choice at lunch between visiting a dating website, or visiting a competitor's website. If you find that you are putting the company first, than you are practicing corporate idolatry.

I don't think the corporate world is a den of evil. Yes, there are companies that do unconscionable things, such as making children's toys with toxic substances like lead or cadmium. Most of us are not faced with those kinds of choices. But we are faced with decisions about when to launch a product, how much to invest in quality control, or how much to tell a prospective customer. What if the path that is better for the customer will cost the company more money? And we have a choice whether to accept that extra assignment that will mean a lot of night and weekend work.

People-first values would say to do what is better for the customers, but doing what is best for the company says that costs should be minimized. People-first values say that it is ok to say no to extra work; doing what is best for the company says that we should do what it takes to say yes to every request. Often, making the quarterly number is a higher priority than the desires of customers or the welfare of employees. This is not done out of evil or ill will on the part of the company--it is an institution, with certain built-in priorities. One of the secrets to keeping to a people-first life is to understand why corporations behave the way they do.

Chapter 2 Questions & Tips

1. Take a moment to reflect on your values, goals, and passions. What is most important to you?
2. What is the biggest influence on how you spend your time?
3. What institutions influence your life? How important is it to support the institution versus your personal needs or the needs of your family?
4. If an outsider could watch everything you do, every decision you make about how to spend your time, how would they rank the following priorities for your life?

    a. Personal health
    b. Personal advancement
    c. The welfare of the company
    d. The welfare of your customers and coworkers
    e. Your family
    f. Dating/connecting with friends outside of work
    g. Your home

CHAPTER 3
The Corporation—
The *Real* American Idol

When I was working like crazy at a genomics company. I really loved it for the first few years. We were the first company to come out with a product for testing 10,000 genetic markers at once. What does that mean? A study that formerly would have taken two years could be completed in just a few months, making it faster and less expensive to identify gene variants that cause disease. In the first year after product launch, there were several impactful publications. In 2006, two years after the product launch, there were fifty-two publications using my product, compared to three from the competitor. This difference led to the creation of my favorite T-shirt of all time, which had a side-by-side comparison of the publication lists. I thought I was being paid a lot of money to change the world. But I had it wrong. I was being paid a lot of money to help the company make a lot of money.

Is a thunderstorm evil? You might think it is if you don't understand how it works. The noise, the lighting, the destructive power can be frightening and dangerous. Is a thunderstorm good? You might think it is, considering the life-giving rain. When faced with the unknown, the mind naturally creates a story to explain what is happening. And when we don't have all of the information, our imagination fills in the blanks, colored by our hopes and fears. Of course a thunderstorm is neither good nor evil, it just is.

And so it goes with corporations; they are neither good nor evil, as they are incapable of any independent moral agency. A corporation can do "good" things like donating money to flood victims, or "bad" things like polluting a river with toxic chemicals. But good and bad are labels added by people and are not necessarily drivers of the company decisions. For example, the oil company Texaco donated money for sixty-three years to allow radio broadcasts of the Metropolitan Opera (a good thing), but the sponsorship also served to help repair the company's reputation damaged by its support for Nazi Germany (a bad thing).[19] A corporation is an institution, and like all institutions its primary mission is to perpetuate itself.

In my opinion, corporations are the most efficient way to create products and services. They create wealth, provide jobs, and drive innovation. And they aren't going anywhere. But what is a corporation?

In the words of Chief Justice John Marshall, "a corporation is an artificial being, invisible, intangible, and existing only in contemplation of the law."[20] Later in the chapter, we will get into more of the legal mumbo jumbo, history, and technical details of corporations. But for now, let's contemplate the corporation as an intangible entity. It is striking to me how it resembles the following definition of a pagan idol.

Reverend Carlton Wynne of the Westminster Theological Seminary writes that idols in the Bible have personhood, are thought to have power, and have the ability to both accept sacrifices and bless supplicants.[21] Corporations meet all three of these criteria: by law they are artificial persons, they have the power to change the world, and employees regularly make sacrifices for the company, which are rewarded with bonuses.

Corporations are fantastic at creating goods and services—they enlist cooperation on a level not possible with any other system. However, even Adam Smith, who coined the term "The Invisible Hand Of the Market" understood that free markets were good for maximizing economic value, not moral value. A corporation is created to make money—that is, increase revenue and minimize costs. Just as a real person will strive to survive and thrive in the fiercely competitive natural world, the artificial person seeks to survive and thrive in the highly competitive economy. But there is one key difference: a living person's struggle for survival is tempered by our capacity for moral reasoning, while a corporation itself is incapable of any moral judgments, or any sense of right and wrong.

Let me give you an example that seems obvious today: child labor. In the United States, the first state to make child labor illegal was Massachusetts in 1832. At the federal level, child labor was not illegal until 1938. So what happened in between? According to The Child Education Labor Project, "Growing opposition to child labor in the North caused many factories to move to the South. By 1900, states varied considerably in whether they had child labor standards and in their content and degree of enforcement."[22]

Presumably child labor was less expensive or more productive than adult labor. So a factory in a state where child labor was illegal was at a disadvantage when compared to a factory in a state that permitted child labor. Based on the drive to increase profits, a strong business case could be made to move the factory. In my experience, if the only reason not to do something is a morality-based argument, a numbers-based business case will win, especially if inaction could threaten the future viability of the company.

Now, I grant that some companies have cultures that do try to adhere to standards other than the numbers alone. I reject the notion that there are "good" companies on the same grounds that I reject the concept of "evil" companies. But whatever company you are in, I would not trust them to set my moral compass. They simply cannot detect moral issues. Asking a company to do the right thing is like asking a blind person to pick out the blue shirt. They can pick a shirt based on size or texture, or maybe even a label that says "blue" in braille. But they do not have the sensory apparatus to know the difference between blue and red.

Only people are capable of moral and ethical judgments. One aspect of idolatry is blind obedience. To blindly follow an institution that is incapable of moral judgment opens the door to acting in a way that runs counter to your core, people-first values.

Punishment by Arbitrary Rules

Institutions and organizations operate by rules. When you work for a company, you are implicitly agreeing to be governed by those rules. It is tempting to think that hard work and good results are sufficient for success. Unfortunately, they are not. There are many factors beyond your control that may limit your success. I'll illustrate this point with an example from the 2012 London Olympics.

American gymnast Jordyn Wieber was the favorite to win the gold medal. After training for most of her life and getting the fourth best score in the overall gymnastics competition, she was not able to compete in the finals.[23] I am fascinated by the psychological aspects of sports—who can outperform under pressure, and who will choke? So when I heard that Wieber was out, I watched the replay, waiting for the choke that never came.

She made a few mistakes, but she was good. And she was out because the rules said that no country could have more than two competitors in the final. There was a storm of analysis about the coaching and scoring decisions that may have cost her, but her coach, John Geddert, said it best: "She has trained her entire life for this day and to have it turn out anything less than she deserves is going to be devastating. She has waited her entire career for this. She is happy for her teammates and disappointed that she doesn't get (to) move on."

Many of us work for years at a company, perform at a high level, and then feel unrecognized or unrewarded for our efforts. Wieber's failure to advance teaches several lessons to advance has lessons for those of us navigating a career in the corporate world.

Lesson 1: There are only so many spots at the top

Wieber's performance was great—fourth overall—but the rules allow only two from a given country. The same holds true in the corporate world. There are fewer and fewer positions at higher levels in the company, especially in management. And being good is not enough.

Lesson 2: Not everyone who is worthy gets to move up

There were ninety-eight women who qualified to compete in gymnastics in London, most of whom knew ahead of time that they had little chance to make the final twenty-four, much less compete for a medal. But these women were the best in their respective countries, and they trained hard to get where they were. Jordyn Wieber was not the only woman who was prevented from competing in the final round because two teammates scored better. Three others also missed the finals because they were third in their country.[24] These women needed to abide by an arbitrary set of rules. And if the rules had been different, then four different women would have been excluded from the all around competition.

Lesson 3: The rules are not designed with you in mind

The organizers made the rules to get as many viewers as possible.

Tim Daggett, the TV commentator, said it was inconceivable that Wieber would not be in the finals, especially when she made no major errors. But the event went on without her, and the ratings were good. But the consequences for Wieber were huge, in terms of lost endorsements and broken dreams.

In my career, it was inconceivable to some people that I would be laid off, given everything I had accomplished at the company. But I was let go, and the company went on.

Lesson 4: Sometimes small things outside your control can make a big difference

Was Wieber underscored on the floor and beam as some suggested? Did the coaches put her at a disadvantage by not having her go last? Probably. If she hadn't made a few small mistakes, it wouldn't have made a difference. But this time maybe it did. Similarly at work, a minor mistake could happen at exactly the wrong time. The corporate world can be a "what have you done for me lately" place. After years of hard work, you can still be heavily penalized if the mistake happens just when that rare window of opportunity opens.

Lesson 5: Sacrifice is a certainty, victory a rarity

For those who choose to work extreme hours, sacrificing family time is a certainty. For an Olympic athlete, the sacrifice brings the opportunity for greatness. But there can be only one Olympic champion. For most people, the experience of being there is a victory in itself. (And with 150,000 condoms distributed in the Olympic Village, there seems to be plenty of rewards for showing up.)[25]

When I first started working at a certain company, everyone kept congratulating me for being hired, as if it was privilege to be there. And given how hot the company was at the time, I can understand where that was coming from. It was perceived as an opportunity for greatness. By business standards, I certainly won the gold a few years later when my product had a monster year. I had sacrificed big and won big. But unlike the Olympics, the competition did not end. There were more goals, more numbers to make, and a perceived need for more sacrifice.

Corporate Guts

Understanding the nature and values of your corporate employer is a key step towards achieving life balance. Dictionary.com defines a corporation as follows: *An **association of individuals**, **created by law**, having a **continuous existence independent of its members, and powers and liabilities distinct from those of its members**.* Let's look at the four key ideas in more depth.

Association of individuals: When a group of people are together, it is natural for a culture to form. Culture provides the norms of acceptable behavior, and is a huge influence on how we are expected to act at work.

Created by law: Ultimately, what a corporation can and cannot do is defined by local, state, federal, and international law. A simple example is minimum wage—depending on where someone is working, his or her minimum pay is a function of local law. A company may choose to pay more, but it isn't *required* to do so.

I interviewed "Bill," who told me that he was part of a group that was spun out as an independent company. Bill thought the whole exercise was motivated by "tax evasion." I asked Bill to elaborate. "There is no revenue stream [in the spinout company], certainly nothing equal to the revenue of the company left behind. I can't really fault the company. I fault the SEC. They had to decide if this was really a tax-free spin off."

I agree with Bill's analysis. The government blessed the decision, and Bill told me that if the SEC had said no, "they probably wouldn't have done the spin off. They probably would have laid everyone off, which actually would have been better career wise for [the employees]. Now they are in a death spiral with this company. I talk to some of them, and some are curiously optimistic. They are under the spell."

Continuous existence independent of its members: Would it surprise you to learn that one of the first corporations in the world was a copper mine in Sweden that operated from at least the year 1080 until 1992? The business was set up to be a distinct entity from its founding members, and it certainly was successful outliving them.

Powers and liabilities distinct from members: A corporation can enter contracts, be sued, and in some cases be held criminally liable in a distinct and separate way from its employees or investors. Many corporations provided limited liability for its investors, meaning that no money beyond the initial investment was at risk.

Again as a simple example, I used to get my paycheck directly from a company bank account, and not from an individual's bank account. Of course a company cannot issue a check (or do anything else) without an actual person doing the work. This leads to many circumstances where a person is acting or speaking in the name of the company. Not a problem in and of itself, until that speech starts to conflict with your internal value system.

I asked many people I interviewed if they were ever in a situation where they had to make a trade off between being straight with a customer and protecting the company. Here is a typical answer, this one from Matthew, a twenty-year software employee and a Buddhist. "I do that every day. I deal with customer issues that are unresolvable, or [are only resolvable] eighteen months in the future. We are encouraged to be relatively straight with them and also to not bad mouth the company. As a representative of the company, we have a certain obligation. It is why you get the paycheck. I have had one or two situations that had to do with directly lying to a customer. It came back and caused a huge headache."

Matthew's last point is worth elaboration. Lying to customers is often a bad business strategy, but the criteria for what speech is permissible varies greatly between company cultures. One company may favor transparency to customers, while another will spin the truth almost beyond recognition.

A Lesson from Biscuits

In his book, *The Pleasures and Sorrows of Work*, philosopher Alain De Botton illustrates how idolatry and non-idolatry both exist in the English company United Biscuits. He describes the development, marketing, and manufacturing of "The Moment," a round chocolate covered biscuit designed to address the yearning of low-income mothers for more "me-time."[26]

Without using the word "idolatry" he describes a corporate office where employees are motivated to surrender their lives/

time to the ideal of helping the mothers find a moment of peace in their hectic lives. According to De Botton, "the leaders at the biscuit company harboured no doubt as to which divinity they were worshipping." Even the investors would "genuflect before pastry."[27] There were "no jokes at any biscuit's expense." He goes as far as to "wish a plague on the house of biscuits so its directors might tremble before the right gods."

It's easy for outsiders like De Botton to poke fun at the people working in marketing and the corporate office because they haven't walked in those shoes. From the inside, it seems natural. I was amazed to read that those biscuit marketers (okay, cookie marketers to those of us on the other side of the pond) had the same desire to change the world that I did in the biotech industry. At least that is the side they showed to De Botton.

But after initially opining the triviality and wasted labor going into making a sugary snack, De Botton gets a glimpse of the economic realities that drive a business. He visits the factory in Belgium where The Moment is manufactured. Most of the other factories in the area have been shut down, and unemployment is rampant. The plant manager is dedicated to his job and his employees. Although the company had enjoyed a number of years of profit, it remained vulnerable to a fierce competitor and changing market conditions. A change in the balance sheet could lead its owner, Blackstone, to close the factory. Jobs in marketing that are initially viewed as meaningless and trivial are recast in a new light—a fight for subsistence. A change in manufacturing productivity or a failed marketing campaign could lead to a dramatically lower quality of life for the employees. They live in a world where it is understood that machines will replace people in the relentless drive for cost savings.

We all need money for survival. For the corporate idol worshipper, at some point a line was crossed between being a serious, dedicated professional, and surrendering weekends and evenings to the company. That is the line where healthy company loyalty morphs into corporate idolatry. The trouble is, it is hard to notice our immediate environment.

The Importance of Shared Values

The writer David Foster opened his 2005 Kenyon Commencement address with this story: an older fish said to two younger fish, "Morning boys. How's the water?" After he swam away, one fish looked at the other and said, "What the hell is water?"[28] Love the story, because it captures a truism—we don't notice something we are immersed in. Corporate culture is the same way.

Corporate culture is defined as the shared values, traditions, customs, philosophy, and policies of a corporation. The culture brings the professional atmosphere to a company, and it affects the behavior and performance of the people who work there.[29]

When I was a product manager, we used to grill new employees about our products to get an outside perspective before they absorbed the biases of our organization. One of the reasons a new job is stressful is that we have not yet learned all of the unwritten social rules.

In their book *In Search of Excellence*, Tom Peters and Robert Waterman argue that great companies have strong values, which are transmitted not through "written procedures" but through stories, myths, legends and metaphors."[30] This rings true for me, based both on my own experience and from stories I heard while conducting interviews for the book. For example, when I asked about company values, people started talking about the bullet points in the employee handbook and were quick to point out that no one paid attention to them. But when I asked for stories, I quickly learned what their company stood for.

For example, when I heard a story about the sales rep who drove a microarray scanner across Europe during the Christmas shutdown and got the customer to unlock his building and take delivery so that the company could recognize the revenue. The sales rep was recognized for helping the company "make its numbers." This story quickly taught new employees an important lesson about the company values – people who sacrifice personal time to help the company make its quarterly number will be recognized and rewarded. Of course the sales rep got a commission check, and it could be argued that he was simply acting in his own self-interest.

But self-interest certainly was not a factor in a story I heard from a former employee of Amersham. In the 1990s, Amersham was one of the few companies where researchers could order radioactive labels, which where used for time-sensitive experiments. An Amersham alum laughed fondly as he told me the story. "Something went wrong with the [nuclear] reactor and the people on the night shift had to run into the reactor to get some stuff [so that it could ship to the customer on time.] They got ten times the dose they legally should have. ... It wasn't driven by commercial gain. It was driven by 'oh we've got to do a good job.'" It was clear that the story was told often, and is the type of myth that helps propagate company values. Amersham was a company that valued always getting the customers their order on time.

"Values" is a term that is often used to describe corporate culture. I find the McKinsey 7S Framework particularly relevant model for organizational behavior. (See Figure 3.1) It categorizes seven elements that together categorize a company: Strategy, Structure, Systems, Shared Values, Skills, Style, Staff.

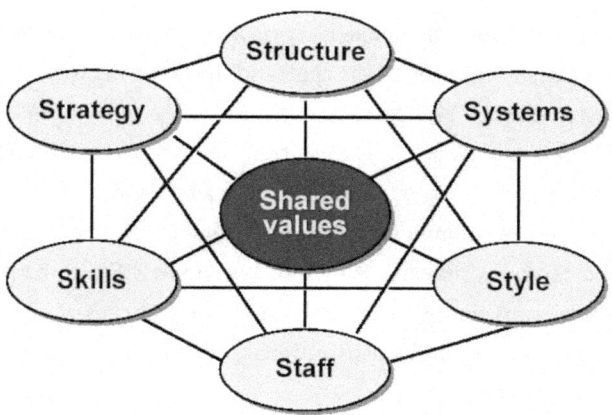

Figure 3.1. The McKinsey 7S model. Shared values are placed in the middle because they influence how the other six elements are executed.

"Shared values" are placed in the center because they touch and define the boundaries of all other aspects of the business, just as personal values touch and define the boundaries of behavior in a person. Shared values are intangible, and are inferred by how people in the company make decisions. Real change in an organization will not happen unless the shared values of the company change. Let me give you an example.

I interviewed multiple people from a Silicon Valley company about its transition from a small to a medium-sized company as its revenue surpassed $250 million dollars annually. The company was now so large that the ad-hoc decision making was no longer effective, and product development was impeded by political infighting. The company sought to solve the problem through systems and staff. It hired a consulting company to deploy a new product development governance system. The system worked beautifully for a year—the product launches were streamlined, and the company had groundbreaking launches in instrumentation, software, and related accessories. Customers were happy, revenues went through the roof, and the company was considered best in class by Wall Street.

But it didn't last. The executive running product development was demoted, and soon left the company. Within a year or two product development once again became political and ineffective, and revenues suffered. Why did this happen? From the perspective of someone who was caught in the trenches at the time, it made no sense and wasn't rational. But in the context of shared values, it does.

The values of the organization (propagated by the founder/CEO) did not reward operational issues or believe in customer feedback. There was a mythical belief that all the company needed to do was to create more powerful hardware and the customers would love it. The CEO had a vision of the world and thought development resources should be concentrated on pushing the core technology, as opposed to the usability features requested by customers. And his vision was shared by a significant portion of the executive team, who were hired and promoted for that very reason.

In summary, it did no good to have a system of development checkpoints if people could go directly to the CEO to approve projects. The core values of the company remained aligned with the CEO's vision. These values led the executives to interpret the financial success as something that occurred in spite of the new system, instead of because of it. For the record, the company went through a series of layoffs as the core technology was surpassed by newer innovations in the market. The company continues to struggle, now a fraction of its former size.

The Number One Value—People First

Tom Peters' book, *In Search of Excellence*, introduced the McKinsey 7S model to the broader business community when it was first published in 1982. Peters argues (as do many others) that strong company values give a competitive business advantage. The top companies "create broad, uplifting, shared culture," which allows them to " extract extraordinary contributions from very large numbers of people" because they share "a sense of highly valued purpose."[31]

This rings true for me, both from my own experience and from many of the interviews I conducted for the book. When people described their best work experiences, often they pointed to a time when everyone in the company was aligned around a clear set of goals. A director of research and development describes her best work experiences.

*There were stages in my job where I loved my work. I would get in early, I would stay late, [and] I thoroughly enjoyed it. I thought I was making a contribution, and it all felt right to me. I thought about what made it good. I was really **clear in my scientific heart**: we had strengths to address what we were going after. My training as a scientist [told me that] the company had resources. It **felt like we were aligned** with the goals of the company.*

On a practical level, shared values facilitate decision making. According to Peters, excellent companies tend not to provide detailed procedures because "people way down the line know what they are supposed to do in most situations because the handful of guiding values is crystal clear." In contrast, Peters sites the difficulty of making decisions at a large company put together by a series of mergers. "The top people are inundated with trivia because there are no cultural norms." Poor companies with strong cultures tend to focus on politics or "the numbers, ... rather than the on the product and the people who make and sell it."[32]

In a sense, the "excellent" companies showed people-first values, in that they empowered people lower down the line to make decisions, whereas the other companies focused on numbers instead of people and had a more hierarchical culture. In my opinion, it is the people-first values that are a key differentiator of organizational success

In his book *The Loyalty Effect*, Frederick Reichheld, head of Bain Consulting's loyalty practice and inventor of the Net Promoter Score, has built a career showing that businesses that put people first have better financial returns, at least in certain industries. Reishheld argues that often a loyalty culture (i.e., one that values long term relationships with employees, customers, and investors), is a productive business strategy. For example, he shows that State Farm Insurance has an advantage over its competitors because it has found ways to retain agents longer, and these older agents bring in more business.[33]

The Loyalty Effect paints a very favorable view of the fast food company Chick-Fil-A for its people-first values, especially with regard to the way it compensates managers and employees in a way that encourages low-turnover. He goes so far as to say that Chick-Fil-A's takes a "Golden Rule approach to business." He calls the founding CEO Truett Cathy (father of current CEO Dan Cathy) "so earnest a Christian that all Chick-Fil-A stores are closed on Sundays which makes their financial success all the more impressive."[34] I agree with Reishheld's further observation that being closed on Sundays may be an advantage for attracting talent that doesn't want to work seven days a week. I would add that because the Sunday closure is a global company rule, no one person can gain competitive advantage for putting in the extra hours on a Sunday.

Reishheld argues that the financial advantages of a loyalty culture are not universal—it depends very much on the type of industry. "Commodity suppliers like oil companies and certain high-tech businesses where technological breakthroughs can overwhelm customer relationships are examples of companies were loyalty economics can make a difference, but probably not a decisive difference."[35]

From my experience in the genomics industry, the dollars followed the latest technology and seemed to be largely independent of how well those companies treated either their customers or employees. In fact, I think the technology superiority bred a certain arrogance, which came back to haunt the companies when the next technology came down the road.

A Public Company's Interests Are Not Yours

Reishheld explains the impact of company ownership on its culture. Public companies are much more prone to short-term, numbers-based decision making than private ownership. "The average public company in the United States now suffers investor churn of more than 50% per year."[36] In other words, half of a company's stock will be bought and sold in less than twelve months, and those owners *only* care about short term results since they will not be owners a year from now.

Such transient corporate owners are in a position to demand changes that increase short-term profits. For example, layoffs and cuts to R&D spending are positive for the balance sheet, but may or may not be the correct prescription for long-term growth.[37]

It is against this headwind of numbers-based drivers that each of us in the corporate world must contend with as we make decisions day to day. Sound like a stretch? Not to Buzz Patterson, a former vice president of Human Resources.

I came home after a layoff of hundreds and hundreds of people. Fourth round. I told my wife, 'I feel like a collaborator in a Nazi concentration camp.' We could have made other choices, like a 15% pay cut and lay off half as many people. ... I got sick of that moral choice of depriving people of their jobs and being in charge of doing it.

Buzz was operating at the intersection of his people-first value system and the company imperative to save money. I am not in a position to judge whether this cost savings was necessary for the survival of the company, but in many cases it is. Layoffs are an unpleasant reality of the business world. Buzz was uncomfortable because he felt they were excessive. The answer for him was to leave that company and find another environment. Another company may have elected to follow his preferred approach of a salary cut, as Hewlett-Packard did in 2012.[38]

This is a theme we will see again and again—much of what happens in the corporate world is beyond your power to control. Once you accept this, you will be in a better position to find a solution that works for you. And no, it doesn't necessarily mean leaving the corporate world.

Corporate Idolatry Versus Business Ethics

As I wrote earlier in the book, idolatry carries a strong negative connotation because it is considered one of the worst sins. According to traditional Judaism, for example, idolatry is considered as bad as murder or incest. I think some people recoil when I use the term corporate idolatry because they work for a good company and see themselves as making ethical decisions at work. So let me spend a moment to explain how business ethics do and do not correlate with idolatry.

Business ethics usually covers behavior involving theft, fraud, and lying to customers. I think it is fair to say that if someone consistently makes unethical business decisions, they follow a value system that violates the Golden Rule and are therefore committing idolatry. Remember, the Golden Rule says that we should put other people first, as opposed to the company or ourselves.

But there is a class of behavior that is not unethical that I still consider corporate idolatry—chronic overwork, particularly by choice.

What happens to people who are chronically overworked? They more frequently make mistakes, have higher rates of injury and depression, and lower life satisfaction.[39] In other words, chronic overwork violates the Rule Of Self Preservation, which makes it another form of idolatry.

Statistics aside, when someone tells you they are working too much, they are describing a stressful, unhappy life. I asked Elaine, a former general manager of a high profile business division, what her life was like when the business was struggling in the market. "It was like hell. I don't know any other way to put it."

Hell indeed.

Idolatry and Hierarchy

In his article "What Is So Terrible About Idolatry?" Rabbi Tzvi Freeman connects a culture of idolatry to the dangers of hierarchy. "[In the pagan world] rulers found that a good mix of secret knowledge and convenient mythology could be an instrument of power over the populace; that by controlling the flow of knowledge they were able to hold the people in awe and obedience."[40]

Leadership guru Tom Peters also wrote of the dangers of hierarchy in his book *In Search of Excellence*. Peters found that "excellent" companies had strong central values which brought the organization cohesion. Peters rightly points out that people crave meaning in their lives, and a company that can provide its employees meaning will motivate them to work harder.

But Peters also recognizes the danger and downside of this dynamic for individual employees. "So strong is the need for meaning in fact that most people will yield a fair degree of latitude or freedom to institutions that give it to them." He goes on to argue that the unscrupulous will use the drive for meaning as a means to exert power for its own sake.[41]

Don't get me wrong, I'm not arguing that everyone in company management abuses their power or is only in it for the money. And I'm also not arguing that everyone else is caught up in the company mystique. But at the same time, we cannot pretend that those dynamics don't exist.

The Main Drivers of Corporate Idolatry

Earlier in the chapter, I argued that corporate idolatry is not the same thing as unethical business behavior. However, there is significant overlap.

Linda Treviño, one of the leaders in the field of business ethics, and colleagues did a meta-analysis of 136 prior publications studying the causes of unethical behavior, with a total sample size of 43,914 people.[42] Not surprisingly, any attempt to quantify human behavior is complicated. Nevertheless, there are enough people to do some real statistics, and what the framework she provided helped me understand the interviews I conducted as background for this book. Treviño found that Unethical decisions at work can be traced to three sources: people, circumstances, and the overall company culture.[43]

People-centric drivers of unethical behavior

According to Treviño, people who primarily look out for number one are more likely to make unethical choices. In addition, the data showed a statistically significant correlation between unethical behavior and the following personality characteristics:

- A relative moral philosophy (i.e., values change with circumstances, which also is one of the key characteristics of idolatry)
- A propensity to manipulate others
- An inability to see a connection between his or her own actions and consequences to other people
- Equally interesting were the characteristics that did not correlate with unethical choices:
- Age
- Gender
- Education
- Level within the organization

The latter finding was particularly disturbing to the authors because "integrity tests are most often used with lower level employees."[44]

Circumstance-centric drivers of unethical behavior

When Treviño's researcher team analyzed what elements in a given situation can lead to an ethical or unethical decision, it basically came down to one thing: how does the decision maker perceive the consequence to other people? With a perception of more immediate, severe, or local consequences, an unethical decision is less likely. Conversely, people are more likely to make an unethical decision if the potential consequences are long term, less severe, or will impact people who are far away. I can't help but notice the similarity to my definition of people-first values.

Cultural drivers of unethical behavior correlate with the values of the organization.

As I have tried to demonstrate throughout this chapter, corporate culture is largely defined by the values and behavior, and certain cultures are more likely to encourage corporate idolatry. In a similar way, Treviño's research has shown that it is possible to identify certain elements of corporate culture that encourage unethical behavior. A company with an "everyone for himself" mentality is much more likely to see unethical behavior than a culture that emphasizes the "wellbeing of multiple stakeholders such as employees, customers and community."[45]

In addition, the presence of a written code of conduct did not correlate with ethical decisions, but "a properly enforced code of conduct can be a powerful influence on unethical choices."[46] In other words, this paper reinforces the notion that actions and behaviors are the only true test of a value system. The authors warn that "performance management systems that reward individual bottom-line achievement (no matter how it is achieved) and that failure to discipline self-serving behavior" are likely to give rise to a climate that tolerates unethical decisions.[47]

As I studied the transcripts from the interviews, I found corporate idolatry is influenced by the same three things: people, circumstances, and corporate culture. The details, however, are different. For example, while Treviño found that age does not correlate with ethical behavior, it does correlate with corporate idolatry.

Chapter 3 Questions & Tips

1. What are the values of your company, and how do they impact how employees and executives act, dress, and talk?

2. What are the stories, myths, and legends at your company, and how do they guide how you make decisions?

3. What are the stories passed down in your company, and what do these "myths" tell you about the company values?

4. What are the people, circumstances, and elements of company culture that influence your work-life balance? Which of these things can you control?

PART 2
Living With Corporate Idolatry

CHAPTER 4

Who To Trust— the Scorpion, the Fox, or the Wolf?

When I was younger, my future wife and I decided to hike between two mountain lakes in the high country of Yosemite National Park. There was no trail connecting the two. It didn't seem like a big deal before we started. That morning after breakfast, I asked the waiter where we should hike. He suggested an informal path down a mile or so of dry creek bed. The course looked pretty simple from the starting point, and I could see the destination off in the distance. After an hour of navigating rocky descents, climbing over downed trees, running from bees and freaking out over bear tracks, there was nothing but trees in every direction. If it had not been for my fiancée's good sense of direction, we might still be out there. The waiter didn't mean any harm, but I should have known better. Then again, I was in my twenties.

At work too, an innocent-sounding request or suggestion can send you down a dangerous path, especially if you don't think through the potential consequences. Like most of us who work in the biotech industry in the San Francisco Bay Area, "Vijay" is a transplant, bringing his skills and knowledge to a new land of milk and honey. The land is beautiful, the weather mild, and the spirit is among the most entrepreneurial in the world. The newcomers are willing to brave the occasional earthquake for the opportunity to work at earthshaking companies.

While Silicon Valley is best known for its technology companies—Google, Yahoo, Apple, Hewlett Packard, Intel, and Facebook to name a few—the Bay Area is also home to some of the most cutting edge biotechnology and medical device companies. These companies include Genentech, maker of blockbuster anti-cancer treatments; Gilead, leader in HIV treatments; and Applied Biosystems (now Life Technologies) that invented the technology that sequenced the human genome. The best, brightest, and most ambitious come from all over the world to make their fortune and to make a difference.

It is to this world that Vijay arrived in the late 1990s with his wife, small children, and a Masters in Biology from a leading Indian university. Vijay is about five eight, a bit stout, and an interesting mix of focused intensity and social sensibilities. The job at a small biotechnology company was a great match for his skills. His attention to detail and meticulous record keeping were integral within the regulatory environment, and his "can do" attitude earned him a place on several key projects. Vijay's performance reviews were laudable, and his boss didn't hesitate to pull him into important meetings. The science was interesting, the work rewarding, and it all "felt like an adventure." Life was good for Vijay the first eighteen months, with a promising career and plenty of time to spend at home with his wife and kids. But that changed unexpectedly after he complied with a small, innocent-sounding request.

Vijay did not think much of it when the lead scientist asked him to change the method used to track the inventory of a new product under development. The scientist was the expert, and Vijay rushed the change order through document control in accordance with the governing regulations. It wasn't until the scientist requested a second change that Vijay grew uncomfortable. He discovered a discrepancy in the amount of actual product in inventory versus the amount in the records. The apparent shortfall would have been further exacerbated by a second change in the inventory calculation method, and in fact could be traced to the first change, the one with his name on it.

Vijay's first reaction was fear—*will I be asked to pay for the missing product?* As Vijay learned more about what really happened, his second reaction was surprise. The scientist had been sending the product from inventory to an academic collaborator, didn't have the budget to pay for it, and appeared to be requesting these changes to cover her tracks. And after Vijay went to his manager for help, his third reaction was shock. His manager did not believe him. The manager made Vijay check his work again and again, and then left him on his own to meet with the vice presidents of manufacturing and quality. Leaving a novice to sort out something like this with the VPs is like having a teenager report teacher misconduct, and then explain it to the principal and superintendent without parental support.

Vijay's manager and both vice presidents were friendly and supportive when he talked to them in private. "I was called to present my data. I thought we were working as a team to find a solution. ... The scientist was panicking. She was always asking me what was happening. It was an ISO regulated place, [meaning that any change to manufacturing must be documented in a very specific way and made available to auditors upon request]. You need to follow the paperwork, and [the scientist] didn't have the paperwork. She was afraid she would lose her job."

The scientist looked over Vijay's records in great detail. But whenever other people were around "she would give totally different answers." Vijay was extremely stressed. "I was by myself. I asked my manager to go to the meetings, but she was always 'too busy,' saying that I could handle it myself. Even though she said she would support me 100% on this issue, she never did come with me. It was the beginning of my career, [but] I always followed the process and documented everything. I think they knew the scientist had made a mistake, but from a corporate point of view she was more valuable."

Without someone to rescue him from the trees, Vijay was let go in the next round of layoffs, the only person terminated in his group. "They were trying to protect themselves from being sued for wrongful termination, and didn't want to give me all the pieces of the puzzle. I needed a good reference, and they gave me a good package. They helped me find another job quickly. To this day, I wish I had not been put in that situation."

I asked Vijay what he would have done differently today from a perspective of ten years out. "I would have prevented myself from getting in that situation in the first place." Bingo. Once the situation starts, it is often very stressful, and difficult to resolve. And what was Vijay's big mistake? Trust.

He trusted a person operating under a different value system.

Is Vijay's story the exception or the rule? In my opinion the exception, but common enough that most people can relate.

I came across a fascinating study by Dr. Craig Parks, which indicated that selfless people at work may be disliked by their colleagues almost as much as the slackers.[48] Why would this be the case? Paul Nunes, executive director of research at the Accenture Institute for High Performance, explains the result on the Harvard

Business Review blog as follows: people at work dislike people who deviate from "normal motivations."[49]

> One can't offer a bonus for harder work, because money doesn't seem to matter. Can't punish with extra or unpleasant tasks because this person takes those on willingly for no apparent reasons. A bit of chaos ensues, with this person being considered complicated—or complicating—at best. I think employees most resent having to come up with new ways of influencing these workers because the traditional ones don't work.

The discussion on the HBR blog after the article is fascinating, with strong resonance from several people who felt this finding "explain[s] perfectly" the resentment they feel from coworkers. The mismatch in motivations comes from a mismatch in the underlying values, between an individual's "personal principles" and the culture and values of the corporation.

I found another study that suggested that people who follow the Golden Rule at work may be at a disadvantage. Men who are less agreeable earn 18.3% more than men who are more agreeable, with disagreeable women earning 5.4% more than agreeable women.[50] Vijay's story is certainly consistent with this finding—the less trustworthy person continued to earn a salary, while the person who was helpful was out of a job.

Who to Trust: The Scorpion, the Fox, or the Wolf

From the perspective of many years later, Vijay told me if he had it to do over again, he would have been able to avoid the situation completely. Vijay learned by experience, and now has a story in his head that helps him make better decisions in the future. As I heard more and more stories doing interviews for the book, I started seeing patterns. Certain types of people kept coming up, and I soon found myself characterizing them according to animals from fables and parables.

Fables and parables have survived thousands of years because they communicate true insights about people, morality, and values. I classify the people in the workplace who have a disproportionate impact on trust decisions as Scorpions, Foxes, and Wolves. The three categories are drawn from the parable of the Fox and the Wolf, and the fable of the Scorpion and the Frog, both of which are easy-to-remember stories that teach important lessons about misplaced trust. If you can understand where someone fits in the "SFW" framework, you will have an insight into their priorities and perhaps their underlying values.

The Fox, Scorpion, and Wolf behave in predictable ways that reflect their underlying priorities, and by proxy their value system. Do they put people first? Do they put the company first? Do they put themselves first? If you know someone's priorities, it becomes much easier predict what they will do, and give you a leg up as you decide whether to trust them or not. Let's take a fresh look at Vijay's nemesis, the scientist. Based on the table below, which animal is she?

	Motivated by	Strength	Weakness	Approach
Scorpion	Strict set of ideas	Execution & vision	Inflexible, polarizing	Avoid or exit
Fox	Self advancement	Talking, motivating	Poor execution	Force them to do more, talk less
Wolf	Getting it done for self, company, ideas	Execution, relationships	Too trusting	Cooperate, partner

Table 4.1. Characteristics of the Scorpion, the Fox, and the Wolf

I classify the scientist, as a Scorpion. "Scorpion" is taken from the following fable of the Scorpion and the Frog.

The scorpion asks the frog to bear him across the river on his back. "You must think me a fool," cries the frog. "You'll sting me and I'll die." "Never fear," replies the scorpion. "If I sting you, we both will drown." The frog relents, and takes the scorpion on his back. Halfway across the river, he feels a burning pain and the onset of paralysis. "Why?" he croaks just before going under. "I couldn't help it," replies the scorpion. "It's my nature."[51]

The Scorpion at work has a single-minded vision of the world. Just as the scorpion in the story can't help itself when it stings the frog, the Scorpion at work can't do anything other than act according to their vision, even when it is potentially self-defeating. When you work with a Scorpion, your happiness and needs are not on his or her radar. Chances are, sooner or later you will be stung.

Vijay's Dr. Scorpion believed that her collaboration with the academic was the key to success for the product. Without regard for budget, regulations, or protocol, she made it happen. When things started to go awry, Dr. Scorpion took a significant risk, a bluff that seemed to disregard potential consequences for herself or Vijay. She could have taken a conciliatory tack, blaming the inventory issue on a misunderstanding or honest mistake. Of course this would have required that she admit that she made a mistake, something Scorpions are loth to do in part because they rarely, if ever, think they have made a mistake. Instead, she gave dishonest answers and let Vijay take the consequences.

What is even more striking is that Dr. Scorpion chose the non-cooperative path even though all the data was on the side of Vijay. A Scorpion will tend to ignore data and rely on his or her guiding vision instead. In this case, once it became a "he said, she said," it was necessary for someone to lose their job. It appears that the company kept Dr. Scorpion based on her greater perceived value to the organization.

For those of you who are keeping score and interested in the outcome, the product was a flop in the market. Dr. Scorpion's collaborator would not pay for the product when it finally launched, and bought a cheaper version from a competitor. We don't know if Dr. Scorpion survived the flop in the marketplace, but we can be sure that people in sales and marketing felt her sting before it was over.

Let me be clear about one thing: the Scorpion is not evil, just inflexible. I use Scorpion as a description of a type of behavior to help me figure out a person's motivation, and then to devise a strategy to deal with him or her. A Scorpion is someone who believes something so strongly they can't help but act in a certain way. And once you understand that your co-worker is a Scorpion, it becomes relatively straightforward to predict how they will react to a situation.

Here a Silicon Valley vice president describes what I call a Scorpion:

"People get an evangelical zeal for the cause they are trying to support. [They] almost won't let anything get in their way and will steamroller people to drive for the particular thing they believe in. When you get individuals like that, the battles get certainly very political and end up being very personal as a result, even though the individuals are often quite mild [outside of work]."

"[For example,] when I first got to know [the CEO] in interviews and semi-socially, he could be a very genial, very humorous individual. But then as you began to hold views that were different from his own about how the technology should evolve or [be] rolled out, he would pigeonhole you into being ... either with him or against him. You couldn't disagree with him in any way."

Another VP describes the same CEO in a similar way:

"An innocuous statement suggesting another technology as a possible solution was taken like a dagger to the heart. Moreover, if you presented market data that contradicted his vision for the next step in the technology, his answer was always 'you don't believe.' That lets someone else step up and say 'well I believe.'"

As I relate in Table 1, Scorpions are good at getting things done when they can get people to buy into their vision. Often great leaders like Ghandi, Churchill, and Steve Jobs are Scorpions. They believe so strongly in their vision that they get you to believe. For example, according to biographer Walter Isacson, Jobs had a "reality distortion field."[52] In other words, his vision of the world could distort the truth, to such a degree that he ignored the advice of his family and doctors and did not get his cancer treated for nine months based on a belief that he could cure himself by eating a particular diet. An often a treatable form of cancer was fatal.

The Scorpion is motivated by an overarching vision or idea about how the world should be, and doesn't let reality get in the way. While the vision itself may be positive and something you agree with, the welfare of individual people takes second place to that vision. A Scorpion (and everyone who follows them) can be very successful if his or her idea happens to be correct. But even if the Scorpion is correct, they are difficult to deal with.

Many people react to a Scorpion with a combination of anger, frustration, and fear. Some work frantically, trying to "please" the Scorpion. Others fight the Scorpion, which can take even more effort than trying to appease the Scorpion. It is not uncommon for a Scorpion to develop a following of loyal, devoted people. It is hard to remain neutral when dealing with a Scorpion, and few people understand that the Scorpion does not care about consensus. I suggest that you try to understand a Scorpion if you work with one. Is the vision something you can live with, or is it completely out of line?

If your goal is a people-first lifestyle, in my experience, the only safe way to deal with a Scorpion is to find an exit, for either you or the Scorpion. If a Scorpion is in a position of power, try to move to another part of the company beyond their influence. If you have more power than the Scorpion, *actively* try to limit their power. If a Scorpion is a peer, keep all interactions transactional, document everything, and do not give them any ammunition to use against you.

Surviving the Fox

I define a Fox as someone who is primarily out for his or her self, and has a particular gift of convincing people to act in a certain way. While a Scorpion truly believes in his or her vision, the Fox does not. The Fox is a talker and not a doer. I picked the name based on the fox in Aesop's fable "The Fox and the Crow."[53]

> A Fox once saw a Crow fly off with a piece of cheese in its beak and settle on a branch of a tree. "Good-day, Mistress Crow," he cried. "How well you are looking to-day: how glossy your feathers; how bright your eye. I feel sure your voice must surpass that of other birds, just as your figure does; let me hear but one song from you that I may greet you as the Queen of Birds." The Crow lifted up her head and began to caw her best, but the moment she opened her mouth the piece of cheese fell to the ground, only to be snapped up by Master Fox. "That will do," said he. "That was all I wanted. In exchange for your cheese I will give you a piece of advice for the future: Do not trust flatterers."

A Fox is the type of person who can convince you that "black is white." The Fox in the office can be charming or critical, but is always a master of "upward management." Often a Fox on the rise has a protector in a more senior role in the company.

Now, let's compare Aesop's fox with the following true stories.

Story 1: "Jack," a Director at a national telecommunications company, laments not recognizing that his colleague is a Fox.

My colleague and I were in contention for a promotion. She won. She went overboard to be my buddy and friend, to be helpful. At the same time she was damning me with faint praise all over the company. "Jack is really good at what he does. Jack is a really good leader, meets project deadlines, but ..." That was her technique. It planted enough doubt about me that I wasn't selected. One of my reports who was close to someone in this other woman's department told me about how she did it, how long she did it, how many people she did it with. That was my experience with betrayal. I thought she was my buddy.

Story 2: "Liz," a senior manager in the software industry, describes her friend "Susie" who got ahead at her expense.

[Susie] would present my stuff and her stuff, but would never tell them I generated it. She was very sweet about it, saying things like "I didn't mean it that way." But she did. She accelerated her career that way. She got a lot of visibility by indirectly taking credit for other people's work. I don't know how she made it work. She was very charming and managed her bosses well.

While a Fox can talk you into anything, the great weakness of the Fox is execution. If you don't do the job for her, she can't get it done by herself. Eventually, a Fox will be found out. For example, I asked Liz how she dealt with Susie, who was taking credit for her work.

When someone gets a promotion before me, I don't mind, no sour grapes. But when they lied and cheated and misrepresented themselves, I have more of an issue. You get to a point where it's not benefiting me to get all riled up about it. At a certain level you will be found out. [If you choose to live that way], you will be the one looking over your shoulder waiting to see who [will] stab you.

For the record, Susie was eventually demoted and later let go. Liz was eventually promoted several times, and went on to run a group of more than fifty people.

Another senior marketing manager shared the following with me, which led me to a strategy for dealing with a Fox. Sometimes "the guy who takes the hit is the guy trying to execute on unrealistic, jackass plans. Two to three rounds [of layoffs] later, it eventually gets figured out and cleaned up. In the meantime there is a wake."

So the key to survival is recognizing this dynamic and finding a way to outlast the Fox. A Fox survives by manipulating others, and sometimes this can lead a good person to do things they ordinarily wouldn't do. Often, the person being manipulated is a Wolf.

The Wolf Trusts Too Much

Unlike the Fox and Scorpion, the Wolf puts people first. The Scorpion is someone who is driven by an individual vision of the world, and will "steamroller people" in pursuit of that idea. The Fox puts him or herself first and manipulates others to get ahead. The Wolf tends to take the welfare of other members of the "pack" into account. But the Wolf gets into trouble because he is too trusting. The characteristics of the Wolf come from the parable of the wolf and fox that appears in the Talmud.[54]

One day, the fox suggests to the wolf that he should help a village prepare a festive meal so that afterwards he could share the meal and satisfy his hunger. Yet as soon as the wolf arrived, the villagers drove him off with clubs and stones. The wolf went back to the fox ready to kill, but he allowed the fox to explain himself.

The fox explained that the wolf's father betrayed the villagers' trust by eating everything (and everyone) after they had prepared a meal together some years before. Imagine the stunned look on the wolf's face. Could this be true?

The fox continued. "If you are hungry, I will bring you to a place where you can eat your fill." The wolf followed the fox to a well, attributing that flutter in his gut to hunger. He told himself, The fox so earnestly wants to help me, he must be trying to make up for his earlier mistake. *A rope with a bucket on each end was suspended from a pulley. The fox, without hesitation, jumped into one bucket and dropped into the well. "Why did you go down there?" he asked the fox.*

"Because this is where the great feast is hidden." The fox pointed to a reflection of the moon in the water. "Look at that wheel of cheese!"

At the fox's instruction, the wolf climbed into the remaining bucket at the top of the well, which simultaneously lowered the wolf into the well and raised the fox to the surface. So enthralled was the wolf that he did not immediately recognize his folly. "Where is the food? What have you done to me?" As he departed, the fox left the wolf with this explanation "The righteous is delivered out of his trouble, and the wicked cometh in his stead."

The fox in this story presents a chilling combination of cruelty and persuasiveness. The wolf was lucky to have survived the encounter with the villagers. Yet, he allows himself to get betrayed again, this time at the cost of his life. In my opinion, the wolf made a fatal error when he chose to talk to the fox. The wolf is clearly the stronger animal; he should either have killed the fox outright, or walked away. A wolf's strength is action, a fox's strength is talking.

The CEO As Wolf

The Wolf is a pack animal who is strong, can get things done, but can be a tad too trusting. Let me introduce you to one.

"Harold T. Lobo" comes across as smart, confident, and open, even about his cockiness, which has faded but not disappeared as he approaches sixty. Harry has the pedigree to back it up: a thirty-year history that includes a stint at McKinsey and management positions at a string of successful companies. Unlike some who have come out of consulting, Harry is an effective operational manager who understands what it takes to get things done and how to set the tone in the organizations he leads. Harry describes his motivations:

"In a nutshell, it's about making a difference to whatever organization I am in, and feeling that I am being challenged to learn new things all the time. I've seen too many people who get to the top of their pyramid and then go into takeover mode. [They think] *I don't need to learn any more and I know it all.* But I find myself always learning."

As the CEO in two different organizations, Harry was quite cognizant of the values he wished to instill in the organization. The first part rests on good business practice, setting clear goals, and following through. The second part, he explains, is "how you treat people. I try to treat people how I'd like to be treated myself." According to Harry, most important are "the incredibly small things that give signals about your values." For example, he abolished his dedicated parking space. In addition, he arrived early and made coffee for everyone. Although he didn't realize it till later, this sent a huge signal to the employees. "Wow, we have a CEO who makes the coffee!"

But make no mistake, Harry set a high bar for performance. According to people who worked for him, Harry was direct and could be intimidating. But he was always professional and never personal. So I was surprised to hear Harry say that some people thought him too nice.

On several occasions in my career when in a CEO role, the board took a view that I was being too soft on employees in terms of cost reduction. Part of the role of a non-executive [board member] is to be much more ruthless and much more cold-minded in terms of cost reduction, reducing heads. As a manager you know these people day to day, and you're the one who will be sitting opposite the desk telling them they haven't got a job any more. There were occasions [where they thought] I should be taking a stronger, more disciplinary stance with individuals. I spend more time trying to see things from their point of view. I have met very few individuals—I can count them on one hand—[who were] out to deliberately put themselves ahead or to sabotage other people. Usually it is different views about what is best for the company.

This last passage is telling in several ways. First of all, we can see the tension between Harry's personal values and the value system being pushed by the directors—to focus on numbers and not people. Second, Harry's belief that very few people are deliberately trying to "put themselves ahead" is consistent with a Wolf's propensity to be too trusting. Harry thinks that people just have "different views about what is best for the company." As we discussed earlier, not everyone shares Harry's values about treating others fairly. In addition, "what's best for the company" tends to frame issues in a way that inherently puts "what's best for people" as a lower priority, which is a characteristic of corporate idolatry.

While Harry has a Wolf's bias towards too much trust, he did not get to be CEO without developing methods to identify a Fox and deal with him or her effectively. He shared with me a story about a time he identified a Fox in his organization, and how he then dealt with him.

When Harry started as CEO in his current organization, he was quite deliberate in how he evaluated the people, and was careful not to make quick decisions. Harry described a vice president who initially looked like a star. "Everything was presented very slickly and efficiently. But as I talked to people around the [company], I found that he was managing communication both upwards in the organization and downwards in a very manipulative way, so that he retained a lot of power by being the communications broker. I took action there to actually part company with the individual."

Note that unlike the wolf in the parable of the fox and the wolf, Harry did not have a probation period, or give the fox a chance to gain the upper hand. In the parable, even after he knows the fox is up to no good, the wolf allows himself to be manipulated a second time, at the cost of his life.

What do you think would have happened if Harry had gone to the VP to discuss the situation and ask for a change in behavior?

How Scorpions, Foxes, and Wolves Relate to Idolatry

The chapter primarily describes a way to categorize people into Scorpions, Foxes, and Wolves to help you determine another person's motivations and by proxy their values. (See Figure 4.1).

So what does all this have to do with idolatry? As we saw in Chapter 2, idolatry is defined by actions that do not put people first, and is something one can adopt for personal gain or by mistake. So really, the Scorpion, Fox, Wolf system is something to help you determine the degree to which a colleague is following people-first values, and if they are not, trusting them could lead to an increased risk of corporate idolatry.

Let's review some of the stories—Vijay early in his career was misled by a Scorpion to submit an incorrect method for tracking inventory, which eventually cost him his job. Had Vijay recognized that it was a Scorpion was making the request, he would have been much less likely to comply and could have avoided the problem that led to his dismissal. Plus, Vijay mistakenly thought the company had a value system that would reward people for doing the right thing, when in fact it kept the dishonest person.

We met Liz and Jack who did not recognize the spoor of a Fox, which had negative career consequences, and Harry who did identify a Fox and proactively removed him from the organization. Of course understanding the values of the people you work with is only part of the problem. As the following story illustrates, even the best people working for the most admirable Wolves, are subject to strong influence from both circumstances and the workplace culture.

One senior product manager we'll call "Jill" had a Fox manager who pushed and pushed in private to "get the product out" and then publicly pointed the finger at her when disaster struck. (Disaster in this case meant that the product did not meet the specifications, and the customers were furious.) According to Jill, "it felt crappy to sit there in the room and watch everyone look to my boss to find a solution. They acted like I wasn't there. But later in the meeting there came this moment when my manager gave me a look that seemed to say, *what do I do next?* I looked him in the eye, and although I knew exactly what needed to be done, I said nothing." And the outcome? The Fox was moved to a backwater of the company six weeks later, while Jill delivered a solution and recovered her reputation.

Over the next year, Jill was able to manage the politics much more effectively. While the environment wasn't exactly supportive, it wasn't hostile either. But the story does not end there, because Jill was still in a very poor situation.

Jill's competition released a product that the customers liked better, and her marketing programs and sales pep talks were not going to change that. Circumstances were beyond Jill's control, but she pushed herself to the edge of ruin in a futile effort to regain market leadership.

Jill believed that her heroic efforts could result in a major change in the marketplace. Psychologists call this the "illusion of control." I call it another face of idolatry.

Chapter 4 Questions & Tips

1. What motivates your boss? Is he or she a Scorpion, a Fox, or a Wolf?
2. Who do you trust at work? Is he or she a Scorpion, a Fox, or a Wolf?
3. Is your work nemesis a Scorpion, a Fox, or a Wolf?
4. Think about what you've learned in 1-3. How can this information improve your work circumstances?

CHAPTER 5

The Pivotal Role of Circumstance—Hot Tables and Bad Breaks

Before my first trip to Atlantic City, a fellow graduate student at MIT gave me advice on how to win at craps: "Find a hot table. When the table stops being hot, stop playing and wait for another hot table." I'll be damned if it didn't work, for the most part. I had an amazing series of rolls. Everyone was cheering and this older guy in a brown leather jacket kept slapping me on the back every time I made a point. I remember the feeling of pure elation like it was yesterday. Before long the table turned, and it was really hard for me to stop playing, but thanks to my friend's advice I did. About an hour later I walked by the table again. It was empty. The guy in the leather jacket was walking away, his hands in his pockets and his eyes vacant. It was twenty years before I saw another table that hot.

Is craps luck or skill? The probability experts are all over this type of thing, and they can tell you how much is luck, and which bets maximize the chance of winning. The odds of rolling for thirty minutes without losing can in fact be calculated, and will in fact occur from time to time. If you happen to be playing a hot table, you are in for a great time because everyone is winning. Of course a hot table is very much an exception—most of the time there will be a mixture of winning and losing, where the only control you have is whether to play, and which bets to make.

In my experience, going to work is a lot like a craps game. The day may go really well, or really badly, but most days fall somewhere in between. And like a craps game, there are times when we feel like we are making it happen, when in reality things are beyond our control.

Funny thing about craps, it can seem like you have control, especially after a few of those free drinks. And in fact, studies by Harvard psychologist Ellen Langer have shown that "people tend to throw harder when they need high numbers and softer for low numbers." In other words, people act as if how they throw the dice has an impact on the outcome. This is an example of what Langer calls the **illusion of control**, "the tendency for people to overestimate their ability to control events that they demonstrably have no control over."

According to Langer, the illusion of control arises in recurring situations when routine behaviors in the mind become correlated with a particular outcome. A person whose routine includes one or more of the following is particularly susceptible to the Illusion of Control: [55]

- The exercise of **choice**
- **Competition**
- **Familiarity** with the activity
- **Involvement in decisions**

Does this remind you of the workplace? It does to me, especially the chaotic environments where I was working all the time. It felt like I was making things happen, but most of it was churn.

Now, lets look at what "Patrick," the vice president of development, has to say about managing to the big picture. "It's a best practice to say that [the work will have a large impact.] But if people can't see **reality** beyond the words, it can be counter productive. To say we are changing the landscape of the market is a **stretch** when our competitor has 80% market share. The **reality** is that we are going to try to get market share. It's less exciting, but it reflects **reality** better."

Do any words stand out as you read this? Pat never says illusion, but he sure says reality a lot!

One of the hallmarks of idolatry is embracing illusions to drive behavior. For example, in the ancient world someone would perform a ritual sacrifice to help bring rain. In the modern world, the illusion of control, allows us to think we are influencing the outcome by following a ritual. I think human sacrifice, which was practiced by many idol-worshipping cultures in the ancient world, is an extreme example of throwing the dice hard to get a high number.

Wikipedia lists three reasons why people experience the illusion of control:

1. **As a coping mechanism** to deal with chaotic situations where there is little actual control.[56] I once asked someone working crazy hours if she was having an impact. Her answer: "I couldn't imagine working this hard if it wasn't having an impact."
2. **Our brain is wired to find cause and effect.** For random games like slots or dice, research has shown that people think their actions are influencing the outcome.[57] So at work, where the situations are more complex, it is even easier for us to think that our

actions are having a bigger impact than they really are.

3. **People who see themselves in control are more likely to detect control when it isn't really there.** Ironically, this means that people with more self-control are more susceptible to the illusion of control.

Pat was considered by his peers to be one of the most solid and capable leaders in the company. When one of the products his team developed had technical issues post-launch, Pat took charge.

"I remember working late every night. I remember feeling a sense of my ability to help put this fire out, how my team had a key role. I took it upon myself to not sleep, to work too much, and I basically ended up in the hospital."

Pat had a panic attack in the cafeteria, and was rushed to the hospital with what he thought was a heart attack. The technical issue was resolved several months later.

Do you think those extra hours had a discernable impact on how quickly the problem was solved?

Pat's story reminds me of this story from the Talmud: A father who dresses his son in the finest clothing, provides him with perfume which omits the most beautiful fragrance, places a purse of gold around his neck and tells him to pass by the entrance of the brothel and not to enter. Is it possible in that context for the son not to succumb to temptation and enter into the brothel?[58] Pat is a take-charge person, who wants to do well in his company. Presented with a crisis, the temptation to work all the time to find a solution was overwhelmingly strong.

Similarly, take a smart person who wants to make a difference, and put him or her on the most exciting project at a small company. Is it possible for him or her not to work all the time? Here is how "Alan" describes his experience at a biotech startup.

I loved my work. There were stages in my first two jobs where I loved my work. I would get in early, I would stay late. I thought I was making a contribution and it all felt right to me. What made it good? I was really clear in my scientific heart that we had strengths to address what we were going after. What I knew from my training as a scientist[was that] the company had resources and it really felt like we were aligned with the goals of the company.

Being aligned with the goals of the company and making a difference are two of the most common answers that people gave me when describing a positive work environment. Alan's story brings back memories of the best times of my career. Then Alan talked about his family life.

"I would go home, have dinner, and then the CEO would call me to re-hash strategy." (This was in the pre-Internet dark ages of the mid-90s.) "The CEO later asked if my divorce was from job stress. It wasn't. I was working hard, but that is not what caused my marriage to crumble."

I pressed a bit, because I was skeptical when he said no, and I thought I was going to get a "work ruined my marriage" story. But life is a bit more complicated, and like many divorces, this one seemed to be precipitated by money. In my opinion, he was working long hours because he was in an unhappy marriage.

Let me be clear—I am not saying that everyone who is putting in long hours does so because they are in a troubled relationship. I used to work very long hours, and while it put a strain on my family, I don't think it ever jeopardized the marriage. However, it is worth reflecting as to why one would choose to work over spending time with your family. In times of stress, work can be a haven, especially when things at the workplace are going well.

I would like to say again that being excited about your work and engaged with your company are good things. Company engagement turns into corporate idolatry when work becomes the most important thing in your life at the expense of everything else. Of course most of the time, the workplace is never all good or all bad.

As "Roger," a VP in Silicon Valley put it, "It's a very rare day when you look at your job and someone can say 'this is awesome, everything is fantastic.' No, there are lots of things in there that you'd like to change, but you have to take the whole package."

Roger explained that the change from good to bad can be very gradual. "At some point, you notice the scales have tipped. It is not good enough and I have to move on."

Many people who left a toxic work environment say that the change was long overdue. I'm sure there are many reasons why people wait so long before finding another job—financial, emotional, social. But I wonder if part of the issue is that it takes us a while to realize how bad things have gotten.

From the book *The Invisible Gorilla* by Chabris and Simons, I learned that we notice a lot less than we think we do. You think you'd be aware that two different actors played the same part in a short silent movie. The new actor wore different clothes, different glasses and parted his hair on the opposite side. Seventy percent of people in the study think they would notice the change, but in reality *no one did*.[59] Zip, zero.

If enough of the details are consistent, and we are not expecting a change, the discontinuity fails to register. And when people were warned in advance, it was obvious and everyone saw it.[60]

I think changes at work can happen in a similar way. We don't notice the small changes as they are happening, which means that over time things can change pretty dramatically without our awareness. And when we are stressed and overworked, it is hard to notice anything. One morning I consciously tried to relax in the shower, and I suddenly noticed that the water was too hot. I had been churning on work, and hadn't noticed that my skin was red from the excess heat. But once I relaxed, I got back in the moment and made the water cooler.

Why Good People Are Mired In Bad Situations

She was in the midst of a successful career. She was the rock holding everyone together at work. She'd moved up through the ranks to vice president. And she was crying and battling migraines every morning.

It wasn't always that way.

"Susan Brady" was used to success. She was valedictorian of her high school class in "Nowhereville," NY, which combined with her drive and determination, got her into Cornell University. Sue is tall, and absolutely direct. And her hair is jet black, except when she's too busy to make it to the hairdresser. Then the grey roots start to peak through. After college, Sue worked at IBM in sales, and moved to Austin to work at a small company that made business software.

Sue started as a senior product manager. "It was hard but fun. Everyone was working towards the same goals, and to this day the core group [of us] remain friends. We made some kick-ass products." For five years, the company did well, growing from a few hundred to close to a thousand employees; her career prospered too. But then things changed.

"The management team fell apart, the strategy started to shift, and the company wasn't doing as well. There was a big panic. A lot of us wanted it to be like it was. I wanted to be the one to bring it back. There was a nagging voice in back of my head telling me it was too far gone. I kick myself for working myself to death, giving up my free time on weekends, not pursuing my hobbies, [and not] spending time with my husband."

I asked Sue if she would have stayed if she had not experienced the good times. She laughed. "No, I would have bailed. [In hindsight,] I had an obligation to do a good job, but I did not have an obligation to give up all of my free time to the company."

In Chapter 8: Build Your Community, we will visit Sue again to see how she remained in the corporate world and balanced her life.

Staying in an unhealthy work environment can be a form of corporate idolatry because one is following a value system that prioritizes work over personal health. Several women I interviewed said they felt like they were in an abusive relationship with the company. One woman told me, "[The competition for jobs in the market] makes me feel stuck dependent on the company. The battered wife who keeps on going back and won't leave, sometimes I feel like that."

People I interviewed cited a number of reasons why they don't leave negative work environments. Here are a few of them:

1. **Loyalty to peers or reports**: *I did not have any corporate allegiance. I had personal allegiance to people within the company. I wanted to protect my staff. [Not wanting to] let that team down was part of [why I didn't leave.] I made it my mission to at least try to make their work environment better than mine*

was. It was frustrating because I could only make it so good, could only fix it so much.
2. **Learning** *[The executives] need to find different ways to value people. It's arrogant. I've seen a lot of turnover. The main reason I stayed was I was learning so much. ... I couldn't have asked for a better learning experience the last few years.*
3. **Momentum** *[I was] very well compensated and it's hard to give up a large paycheck. [Leaving] came to mind frequently. One [good] thing would happen—it's never all bad. I'd find some silver lining and choose to think about [how to fix things.]*

While all of these reasons can play into why someone stays in a negative circumstance, the single biggest impact is the stage of your career when you encounter the negative situation.

What the First Job Can Teach You

"Mary Cassidy" could not get out of the academic world fast enough. She went to graduate school for six long years studying oncology. It was not a supportive environment, and the project was difficult. The Ph.D. felt like it had been paid for in blood. On a good project, experiments lead to a clear yes or no answer, allowing the researcher to move on to the next experiment. Ambiguous results are a nightmare—one initial yes, the replicate no, and then a lot of maybes. This led to repeat after repeat, which was both demoralizing and frustrating. Moving from the snows of the Midwest back to San Diego to work at a small but hot biotech company was exciting beyond her wildest expectations.

Mary is tall, with curly dark hair and a serious expression when you first meet her. After a while her bubbly side emerges, a pleasant balance to her focus and determination. She spoke to me with great sincerity and emotion, and she tells the story better than I ever could:

"[At] my first job out of grad school, I was excited and wanted to do well. The culture was a small company feel, everybody knows each other, familyish. Everyone was trying to do the right thing to make the company successful. You wanted to go the extra mile, [because] you were working with your friends. You felt this camaraderie. I was traveling for the first time, yeah! I'll go anywhere yeah! Just all the perks of being in a company versus academia: the money, the bonuses, the 401k—it was so exciting. I felt so successful compared with my Ph.D. Writing emails at night, fixing customer problems, writing customer requirements, [work] fulfilled me to a certain amount. Even now, ten years later I still feel a connection to many of the people I worked with."

Mary's face grew dark as she continued. "When the layoffs hit, it was such a slap in the face. It was really hard. I have very vivid images of the layoffs. I wasn't part of it, but it was a mess. I remember the CSO was crying. Everyone had to get in a room. I remember being up high, looking down and seeing everyone scrambling around in the corridor to see if they were on the list. It was awful."

The layoffs were a wake up call for Mary.

"I was thirty and still single. I thought, 'I'm killing myself for the company, and not getting anywhere in my personal life.' You don't realize that at first, except for Friday nights when you grab a movie, Thai noodles, and sit by yourself. [Then I started to think] 'Wait a minute, I want to get married, have kids, and I'm getting older. I have an awesome apartment downtown and no one to share it with.' I traveled a lot and gained weight, which made it hard to be single. Even if I looked fine, I didn't feel good about myself."

It is perfectly understandable that early in her career, Mary did not understand the business realities, especially coming from a different set of realities. As a science graduate student, she worked independently on her project with a large peer group of fellow grad students to commiserate with. There was no overall institutional loyalty—a graduate student is part of a scientist's lab, who in many cases could care less about what you think of them or the institution. In fact, many graduate advisors hate the institution for all the bureaucracy. Personal identity does not become intertwined with the institution.

A corporation is a completely different environment. It's about making money for the company, and working with other people towards a common goal. At work Mary was surrounded by signals that reinforced her attachment to the company, and she was caught up in the gung-ho attitude of trying to change the world.

The customers were almost all of the top twenty pharmaceutical companies, which reinforced her perception that the company was helping to revolutionize drug discovery. And, these companies were a very lucrative source of revenue. At one point, the stock price was going up 20 to 30 points a day, and everyone was talking about it. You could literally hear people screaming out numbers and cheering from their cubes. One of the founders, whose major contribution at the time was surfing porn sites, was once seen dancing down the hall chanting the company name.

Describing herself at the time, Mary laughs. "I was very green."

For Mary and many others, the president was the embodiment of the company. He was charismatic, smart, and visionary. In monthly company meetings, he would lay out his inspiring vision for how the company was going to change the world, and when he spoke, it was almost impossible not to give him your full attention.

More importantly, the president made an effort to say people's names and say hello in the hallway. Mary describes her memory of the president. "He was almost a father figure, an uncle. He fostered a love of the company, you felt that you belonged."

In many ways, Mary was in a dream job. In her first position out of graduate school, she worked for a small company with exciting products and a charismatic, visionary leader. And the products were making money, a lot of money.

Mary had not done anything wrong. Many people in that circumstance would have been very devoted to the company. I know that I would have been, because that is how my career started. A dream job is a wonderful thing. But if you are not okay without the dream job, you won't be okay with it either.

I interviewed a number of people in HR about this issue. One told me, "It happens all the time. One of the successful rising stars comes in and asks, 'Is this all there is?'" The research is clear: people are happy when they have connections to other people. In spite of her success, Mary felt unfulfilled because she was alone.

The Risk Mary Took

Fast forward ten years. Married now, Mary was several companies down the road, and did not love, or even like, her company. Yet she found herself once again overly devoted.

Mary had grown in seniority, and was managing an experienced team. However, she had not yet made director, which was troubling and painful to her. As was usually the case, Mary was working on the most high profile and high-pressure project in the company. This was no start up, but rather one of the largest in the life sciences research industry. The product was billed as (and in fact was) a game changer in the world of cancer detection.

Challenges presented themselves right away when she came back after four months at home with the baby. Mary's senior employees had been reporting to the director in her absence, and they resisted being pushed back down a level in the hierarchy. What was particularly challenging was a culture of after-hours discussions and meetings, where decisions were often made when she wasn't present, by either her reports or her manager, people who did not share her level of expertise. "Decisions could be made where you wouldn't know [the impact] for a few months. You could really dig yourself in [such that customers would be livid]."

What was worse, Mary had to defend those decisions to the rest of the department. "To sit in all hands meetings where senior managers were pointing fingers, and then to stand up and defend decisions I wasn't making. That got really old. That and the hours, the sheer amount of work. I was putting the kids to bed, and [then working] to midnight every night."

One of Mary's team left for another role in the company, and she was quickly overwhelmed. "I couldn't hire quickly enough. There were a couple of months where I was working eighty-plus hour weeks. I would ask my husband to take the kids to the zoo on Saturday so I could have the whole day to catch up."

Nowhere in this part of the conversation did Mary mention love or devotion to the company. It was no longer about a family atmosphere, or changing the world. In fact, I don't think she even liked the company. Mary was driven by guilt and fear. She worked each night until midnight, and often a full day on Saturday, yet she felt guilty about leaving work at 5:00 p.m. "I think I thought I was going to get fired. It was right after the merger, and there was all this pressure. All these managers from Boston who wanted to know what was going on. I was accountable to all these [new] people. The pressure was crazy." To further compound the stress, Mary was the sole breadwinner. "If I got fired from my job, I didn't see the monthly bills [getting paid]; everyone was on my [health] insurance."

Mary had the option of staying later every night. Because he was unemployed, her husband could have assumed all childcare duties. As it was, he shouldered most of them. "If I would have stayed at work consistently most nights till seven, I would have been able to build those relationships across the company that you need, so they have your back. I saw it happening, but I just couldn't [stay]."

Mary's top priority was the family. She left every day at 5:00 p.m. to make sure she could eat with the kids and put them to bed. "I thought I could make it work. The baby goes to sleep at eight, and I would work till midnight. I kept getting further and further behind, and relationships kept suffering. If I had any free time, I was trying to catch up on some project."

While it is likely that staying until 7:00 p.m. every night may have eased the work-related guilt and facilitated the relationships with R&D, I doubt it would have changed Mary's overall level of happiness or health. In fact, Mary would have had little time to see her family, which would have engendered guilt of another kind. To her credit, Mary continued to put her family first. At the same time, she was prioritizing the company over her health, which was not sustainable. People-first values mean taking care of your health first and foremost.

Things finally came to a head when Mary tearfully told her boss that enough was enough. "I said, 'If that is really what you want me to do, I am not sure I'm the right person for that job.' At the time you don't expect you were going to say those words, and when you walk out you say, 'shit, I'm basically getting myself fired.' In another way you feel good that you finally stood up for yourself." To his credit, Mary's boss found her another position in the organization, one that was protected from an upcoming round of layoffs.

In her new position at the company as a technical writer, Mary's life changed dramatically for the better. She started working normal hours, and was recognized and appreciated for her work. Interestingly, it took her about three months to accept the new lifestyle. "I kept asking myself when is it going to get crazy again." Now she wishes she had made the move earlier. "I just feel like I suffered for longer than I needed to [in my previous position]. This year has been a recovery year. I haven't felt guilty about the number of hours I work. If I leave at three to work out and get the kids, I don't feel guilty about it. I was getting my work done, and was still moving the position forward."

It sounds like more than just moving forward: Mary was recognized and complemented by the general manager in the hallway, something that never would have happened in her previous position. Moreover, Mary is still connected to the high profile project, which allows her to leverage her previous experience and contacts.

At the start of this chapter, I wrote about the illusion of control, and how it applies in the workplace. There is so much that happens which is beyond our control, but as humans we are naturally susceptible to the illusion that we can control far more than we actually do. And the consequence for these illusions, are longer hours, higher stress and unnecessary suffering. To paraphrase Viktor Frankl, we cannot control what happens to us, we can only choose how we respond.

Next up, the biggest thing we cannot control—the overall company culture.

Chapter 5 Questions and Tips

1. Where are you in your career? Less than five years, five to ten years or more than ten?

2. How have your priorities changed as you have gotten older? Do you think they may change in the future?

3. Has a work-first value system interfered with other parts of your life, like dating, having kids, or participating in community activities?

CHAPTER 6

Corporate Culture and the Invisible Hand of the Company

The good news: I got the product out on time after leading the team through twelve months of crisis product development. The bad news: it did not perform well in customer hands. The only surprise for me was how surprised senior management seemed to be. Prior to launch, the executives would stop me in the hall to ask if we were on schedule. They did not say, "We will support any decision you make," or "Protect the long term relationship with customers." They reminded me how much revenue was on the line. I loved the attention, and I was going to make sure we delivered what they were asking for.

After launch, I was too depressed to effectively defend myself from the storm of criticism because I felt that I let the company down. What a ridiculous thought. The company isn't alive, so it can't be let down.

What I understand now that I didn't understand then was that the company had a culture of making the date, and if I hadn't been leading the team, someone else would have been. It was expected that vacations would be canceled if need be, and they were. I even called and led a conference call of several hours on the Fourth of July to help the team make the date. I was at a family reunion at a resort in New Mexico, standing outside in the one patch of ground that had two bars of cell coverage—just enough to be heard. If I walked more than ten feet in any direction, it dropped off. It kind of symbolizes the whole project—in theory I could walk anywhere I wanted to. But if I wanted to be heard, I had limited room to maneuver.

Of course none of this absolves me of responsibility for the choices I made. I also don't want to make this seem like a bigger deal than it was. I don't think I or anyone else at the company was involved in the types of major ethical lapses that one reads about on Wall Street or in the Enron case. This was more of the garden variety business, if not quite usual, certainly not all that unusual.

According to a survey by the American Management Association, seventy percent of respondents said that "pressure to meet unrealistic business objectives/deadlines" was one of the top three reasons for unethical conduct, which far outpaced the second most common answer, "desire to further one's career" at thirty nine percent and "to protect one's livelihood" at thirty-four percent.[61] Another survey found that meeting deadlines was second to the need to "follow the boss's directive."[62] These answers have a common theme—compliance, either to peer pressure or to the manager.

The Power Of the Revenue Forecast

The Cambridge dictionary online defines a revenue forecast as "a calculation of the amount of money that a company will receive from sales during a particular period."[63] It is tempting to think that these numbers are scientifically derived and reliable, but often they come from sticking a finger in the air, and are then justified after the fact in Excel.

I used to agonize over my revenue forecasts. I'm sure the scientist in me was holding me back, or rather was driving me to make them incredibly precise. But that didn't make them more accurate. I used to get advice from people in the know like "be confident" and "just list your assumptions." But I never really got it until my very last product forecast.

I presented the forecast on the phone, using a hard copy of the slide deck. It was a routine launch review for a small product, and I had nudged up the numbers since the previous checkpoint due to favorable market conditions. I got a surprising amount of pushback from the executive review committee, but I confidently defended the numbers, citing "changing market conditions." I was really surprised at how excited the execs were as they signed off. The next day I discovered why: finance made an error in the last minute slide preparation, such that the revenue was one hundred times higher than it should have been.

I should have caught the mistake, and earlier in my career I would have panicked and felt really crappy. But that day, I laughed out loud and never said a word to anyone. The bar graph was absurd: one huge bar on the right and a bunch of tiny pancakes to its left. But I was a hero for my rosy prediction of the future.

I finally got it. I was hung up on finding the truth, but there is no truth to be had in a forecast. Predicting the future is impossible. And by changing assumptions, a forecast can be made to say anything.

Forecasting, Soothsaying, and Idolatry

Many dysfunctional companies live and die by the revenue forecast because they can't seem to agree on anything else they stand for. A revenue forecast is an *estimate* of how much money the company will make over a period of time, not a prediction of the future. Yet these companies treat a revenue forecast as an actual prediction.

The medieval Jewish philosopher the Rambam (aka Maimonides) argued that soothsaying, fortune telling, divining, and related "black arts" are forms of idolatry perpetuated by unscrupulous leaders as a means to control other people by fear. The Rambam said, "It is not fitting for the Jews who are wise sages to be drawn into such emptiness."[64] To put it more kindly, he was saying that educated people should know better.

In a similar way, I think that people in the business world should know better than to blindly follow forecasts or other means of predicting the future, which is exactly what professor and former hedge fund manager Nassim Nicholas Taleb argues in his book, *The Black Swan*. Taleb, like the Rambam, marvels that people seem to ignore the terrible track record of those who routinely predict the future and get it wrong.

Taleb uses the example of the black swan as a metaphor. For hundreds of years, bird experts said that black swans do not exist because one had never been seen. Which was true until Europeans reached Australia, where they found many black swans in residence.

Taleb shows that financial analysts have a terrible track record at predicting the future—they are no better than someone who looks just at the last quarter's data and extrapolates. In fact, the analysts tend to follow the herd and are unlikely to make predictions that are outliers.[65] But the biggest events that change history, like the September 11 attack or the fall of the Soviet Union, are almost never predicted.

If the Wall Street experts can't get it right, what chance does the average revenue forecaster have in an average company?

A Dangerous Forecast

I heard a cautionary tale from "George," the former VP of marketing at a mid-sized biotechnology company, about how a bogus forecast helped propagate a disaster. The research department created an elaborate robotic system to streamline the user experience for one of the flagship product lines. After a few experiments, they pronounced it ready to ship to customers, meaning that it did not need to go through a formal development process.

I cringed when I heard the story. Product development is always needed to make a new technology robust enough to work consistently in customer hands.

But "ready for customers" is exactly what the CEO wanted to hear. He was a Scorpion, a "visionary" who felt that the technology should sell itself. The president and CFO were hungry for revenue growth, and via a process that sounds a lot like groupthink, the executive team convinced themselves that "we should be able to make $10M on this product this year." Marketing then back calculated the number of units, service contracts, and consumables that would need to be sold to make the forecast. (As a point of reference, this represented twenty-five percent of the company's projected revenue growth for the year.) When the product ran into development issues, the same executives went on a headhunt to find out where the number came from.

The rest of the company scrambled to fill the $10M revenue hole. Timelines for other products were accelerated, and employees throughout the organization put in long weeks to "make it happen."

Bad management? Sounds like it. But people were not rushing for the door. Inside the asylum, everyone looks sane.

What Happens When a High Integrity CEO Meets Toxic Culture?

If you put a high integrity, fair, and trusted person into a toxic and/or unethical culture, which would win? In other words, will the person change the culture, or will the culture change the person? To what degree can an individual change corporate culture? It's a question we'll come back to multiple times in this chapter.

Let's start with an extreme example: What if Harry T. Lobo, the highly respected and effective CEO we met in Chapter 4, were made the CEO of Goldman Sachs, a company thought by many to have an unethical culture. (Greg Smith's very public resignation from his position as a vice president at Goldman Sachs made public the callus and thoughtless way Goldman treated their clients.)[66]

Harry, who is not known for his modesty, didn't think he could change the company value system. Harry told me, "[It would] depend on the company, and how long the value system existed. Goldman Sachs [is very big and is] proud of the way it operates." Harry explained to me that everyone working there shared those values, and it would be too hard for even the CEO to change the culture. Harry shared his experience changing the culture of the company he is now running.

After becoming CEO, it took Harry five years to change the culture of a mid-sized organization. When he arrived, the company was full of "empire builders," with a "negative, finger pointing, aggressive culture." People who were resistant to the values he was instilling are "no longer around." Harry said that he let this happen over time. As people realized they no longer fit in, they left, and people who espoused the values he was looking for were promoted. This is a common theme I heard throughout the interviews I conducted, and it is well described in the literature—people who fit best with the company's values, whatever they may be, will tend to be promoted more quickly.

So how did Harry respond when he was working as a senior VP in a toxic culture?

Prior to his current (and second) stint as CEO, Harry was the Chief Operating Officer (COO) of a technology company in Silicon Valley. I'll call the company "Scorpco" because the CEO was a Scorpion. During Harry's first year, the company launched a complete upgrade to its platform—software, hardware, peripherals, and third party components. "[We delivered] it all and had successful sales. In most companies, you get paid a big bonus for that. It didn't work that way at Scorpco." Instead, Harry was demoted and left the company a few months later.

The year was difficult—Harry had to defend many decisions publically that he did not agree with. "I'm a firm believer that if you're part of a management team that by whatever mechanism decides on a course of action, it's your duty to carry it out with absolutely the best grace you can. I have always tried to take ownership of that decision, rather than place it as a third party decision."

Harry had a philosophy of long-term objectives, but the company was perpetually focused on the short term. "Sixty percent of revenue came in last forty-eight hours [of the quarter.] It's a crazy way to run a business," Harry told me in an exasperated tone. And the cost was great. According to Harry, "burnout was high" and he felt "sheer exhaustion, both physical and emotional."

I asked if the CEO pressured him by calling him at home.

"No," he said, "the pressure was more subtle and psychological, the 'you're not really up to it' sort of thing." Harry described feeling "bruised and battered," and at times questioned his own competence.

"It's not as if I'm sitting around not thinking about this day in and day out. If it's still not good enough, how the hell can I possibly improve? How can I be getting this wrong with all the work I'm putting in? But then with me the grit and determination comes in, and I say, 'I'm not going to be defeated by this. How *can* I address some of the issues being raised here?' It means either going back to what you were doing with renewed confidence to push it a bit harder, faster. Or you could say, 'Okay, I'm doing something wrong here.'"

In my opinion, those very qualities that made Harry an effective CEO when we first met him—loyalty, tenacity, self confidence—worked against him in this situation. In hindsight, Harry understands that the CEO's growth expectations, based on the greatness of the technology, were not rational. But at the time, when he was in the thick of the situation, it just wasn't possible to see the bigger picture.

And what made it so hard for Harry? He was working in a culture that did not match his values, and he was powerless to change it. For example, Harry believed in long-term relationships with customers, but the company culture prioritized the quarterly number. Let me say that again: Harry T. Lobo, former CEO and extremely effective leader, was unable to change the company culture. A less capable person would have left, but Harry's tenacity and self-confidence led him to stay in a toxic situation.

I have come to believe that it is almost impossible for an individual to change the company culture. Think about it: if it were easy, would so many corporations spend millions on "change management?" For example, Bain executive Frederick Reichheld outlines eight steps towards changing company culture in his book *The Loyalty Effect*, a process that takes years.[67]

So my advice? Don't bother to try to change the company unless:

1. You are CEO.
2. You have the support of the board.
3. You have absolute power to hire and fire people.
4. You are ruthless enough to clean house.

Unless *all four* of these things hold true in your situation, it is beyond your power to change the company culture. Cynical and hopeless? Not at all. It is liberating to accept the truth. The energy going into a futile effort to change the culture can be redirected to your personal life or towards influencing your *local environment* within the company. Or towards finding another place to work. Chapter 9: Paint Your Environment will go into solutions for corporate culture in greater depth.

The Downside to a Free Lunch Culture?

Shortly after the arrival of Marissa Mayer as CEO, Yahoo started giving free lunches to its employees as a means to change the culture and improve morale.[68]

Google, where she worked for many years, is known for having free, very nutritious lunches. It's a great benefit, and while I've never eaten there, I did go to the Califia Café, a great restaurant in Palo Alto, CA started by a former Google chef. The food is fantastic.

By one estimate, Google spent $72 million on food in 2008.[69] Why does Google do that? Does anyone think it's because they care about employees or are being nice? The benefits to Google include higher morale, a stronger culture, a talking point to keep salaries lower,[70] and a way to keep people close to the office.

And it's not just food that Google and other companies offer. According to tech enthusiast Jonathan Strickland, the Googleplex offers on-site haircuts, medical, dry cleaning, laundry, and massages as well as pools, gyms, video games and ping-pong. According to Strickland, the strategy is "keeping the employee workforce in the office more often. Give employees enough reasons to stick around and you'll likely see productivity go up. Why head home when everything you need is at work?"[71]

These perks are one way to address the difficulty of work-life balance by bringing some of the life tasks into the workplace. Is there a downside to this? I think there is. The free perks can make the employee more dependent on the company. If the employee wants to change jobs, they also need to change dentists, dry cleaners, and so on. And, there is less of an opportunity to connect with people outside of the workplace.

The Benefits of Working for an Ethical Company

Throughout much of the chapter, I have argued that it is extremely difficult to change company culture. It's so hard in fact, that I don't think it's worth trying if you aren't the CEO, and even then it may not be possible.

But the good news is that there is a wide range of company cultures. One of the greatest myths about the workplace is that "everyplace is like this." That isn't true. It is true that no place is perfect, but there is a dramatic difference in the ethical climate between companies.

The business ethics literature describes an ethical culture as a company with a focus on the "wellbeing of multiple stakeholders such as employees, customers and community," whereas a culture that encourages unethical decisions has an "everyone for herself" mentality.[72]

And how can you tell which type of company you work for? To state what is probably obvious, one place not to look is the written code of conduct. According to a large statistical meta-analysis of the business ethics literature, the presence of a code of conduct is not correlated with actual behavior in the company. What matters is that the code is enforced uniformly across the organization.[73]

So how are people treated in your company?

Are bullies tolerated? Are vendors treated fairly? Are the leaders held to different standards? Are certain people allowed to get away with swearing while others are not?

The small things matter because they are clues to what will happen when the big things come up.

For a happier, more balanced life, the long-term solution is to separate your identity from the company. More on that in the next chapter. But in the short run, the best answer may be to change companies. In my opinion, all things being equal, it is better to work for a company that treats people well because you will be treated well.

Chapter 6 Questions and Tips

1. What is the culture at your company? Do people brag about working over the weekend? How is someone who doesn't stay late viewed?

2. Where does your company fit on the spectrum from short-term focus to long-term focus?

3. What is the company culture with respect to truth? Is it okay to raise issues, or do they shoot the messenger? How transparent is the company with its customers?

4. Have you ever tried to change the company culture only to have your work undone by someone more senior?

5. In your current company, how are people treated? Who gets ahead? Are senior managers held to the same standards as everyone else?

PART 3
The Post-Idolatry Life

CHAPTER 7
Secure Your Identity

When I finally resigned from the corporate world, I told everyone it was not because of the product, the company, or the people. It was about my personal journey to take care of the kids and to figure out what to do next. I was both lying and telling the truth. In public, management was supportive, but in private, it got nasty. One person, pressuring me to work an additional two months, went so far as to say, "You will never work in this field again if you leave the company in a difficult position." If I'd resigned to work for a competitor, they would have walked me out the door and happily had a beer with me the following week. But to turn my back on the system was heresy.

Leaving the corporate world was not the means to regain control of my life. It was the result of it. I had been living with a reasonably healthy life balance for a few years when I finally resigned. The change for me started when I recognized my corporate idolatry, that I was following company-first values instead of people-first values.

It came down to a fundamental question that I asked myself: who are you? I was a lot of people—a father, husband, son, friend, marketer and scientist. But the one I thought of the most, was the guy who worked for the genomics company. I was the guy who was changing the world. But on a deeper level, I was a guy whose self-worth came from the job.

The first thing I tried, to reduce my hours, was a time management course taught by the American Management Association. I was frantically busy and thought that by managing my time better, my issues would be solved. It was a great class, and I learned two things. I flew to New York City for the class, and was the only person with a high tech job. But everyone in the class had the same personal story: my hobby used to be such and such, but I don't have time for it anymore because of my job. These were people in construction, high school yearbook sales, and in the media. My first lesson: it's not just the high tech industry with an overwork issue. It's everywhere.

The second thing I learned was to be more efficient. Less procrastination, better goal setting, and better prioritization. This class was good. I became more efficient, and my life got better because I was working fewer hours per week. This was great for a few months, but pretty soon I was just as busy. It was a better planned busyness, but my life was once again out of control—all work and no play made Greg an out of shape and crabby boy.

Now, I understand why. The overwork was a symptom, but not the root cause. The root cause was my corporate idolatry. I had adopted and internalized a company-first value system. The company was (unconsciously) the most important thing in my life. So all of the time that I saved from greater efficiency was put back into the company. Things started to change for me when I reconnected with people. And as I reconnected, I shifted my identity.

Stanford Business School professor James G. March describes identity as an expected set of behaviors that apply in certain social situations. Put another way, identity is an automatic pilot that unconsciously guides behavior. An identity is reinforced by the social context that rewards "behavior consistent with the definition of the identity and penalizing behavior inconsistent with behavior."[74]

For example, a parent identity is reinforced by parenting-related activities, such as the appreciative smile that comes from a child when you attend her soccer game. An identity that comes from the company is reinforced daily by the interactions, both positive and negative, that happen at work. Some companies, like Google, go to great lengths to build a company-centric identity of employees from the time of hire.

The First Step to Change Is a Time Audit

While we all have multiple identities, the dominant identity is the one that drives how we spend our time. When I was working ninety hours a week, the last thing I had time to do was to reflect on my life. But if I had, it would have looked something like the pie chart in Figure 1. I still cringe when I see it, because it is a visceral reminder of how tightly my identity was wrapped up in my company.

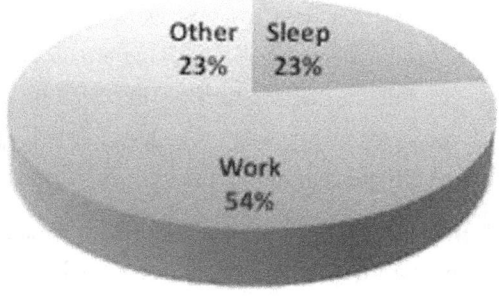

Figure 7.1. Time Profile of a Ninety-Hour Week

The time audit is a very simple way to bucket your time into one of three categories: work, sleep and everything else. (Forget journaling minute to minute, and other complex systems to understand how you spend your time.) Figure 7.1 is a result of a time audit that I gave myself. Here are the three steps to give yourself a time audit:

1. **Calculate the number of hours you sleep.** For the last week, what is the latest time you turned out the light to go to sleep? When did you turn on the light in the morning? This tells you the number of hours you slept. (Note that getting undressed, reading and brushing your teeth do not count as sleep time.)

2. **Calculate the number of hours you work.** What is the time you answer your first email in the morning? What is the time you answer your last email at night? Commute time counts as work. If you eat alone and think about work during meals, count a hundred percent of that time as work. If you ruminate about work during meals with other people, count fifty percent of that time towards work. In fact, if you are thinking about work, checking email, or taking phone calls during an activity (like reading stories to your kids or watching a college football game), count fifty percent of that time as work.

3. **Calculate the "everything else" bucket** using the following formula: Twenty-four minus hours spent sleeping minus hours spent working = everything else. For example, if you sleep 6 hours, and work 12

hours, the formula is 24-6-12=6. Six hours for everything else in your life.

Time is a zero sum game. If you spend time on one thing, it is time not spent on something else. A lot goes in the everything else bucket—cooking, fixing the car, going to the doctor, plus the fun stuff. (I put sex in the sleep bucket because both are so wonderful and both take place in bed.)

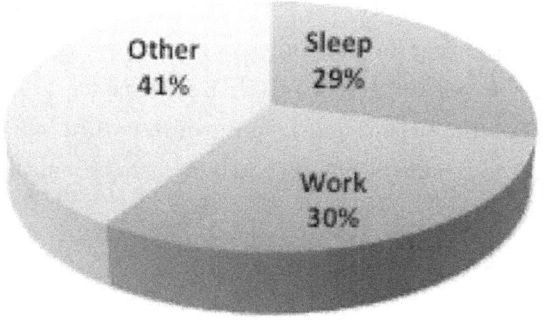

Figure 7.2. A time profile for a fifty-hour week.

An ideal time profile has eight hours each for work, sleep, and everything else. Figure 7.2 shows a very achievable time profile for people in the corporate world, a fifty-hour week. I call this Life Balance, because there is sufficient time for all three components of living.

Jesus of Nazareth said, "Where your treasure is, there your heart will be also."[75] Our greatest treasure is time. How we spend our time tells us what our real values are. When we spend time on one thing, it takes away from something else. The good news is once you understood this dynamic, you gain the power to make real changes.

Don't be discouraged if your life is way out of balance today. The more out of balance you are, the easier it is to make changes that will quickly improve your life. Because you are reading this, you are the type of person who wants to have a balanced life. And in less than a year you can if you follow the steps here and in the following chapters.

Values and Priorities

Moving from a lifestyle of corporate idolatry to Life Balance requires a change in our underlying value system. Figure 7.3 revisits the Values Decisions Cycle from Chapter 2. Our values influence our decisions and actions, which in turn influence our values. And actions we do over and over again become habits.

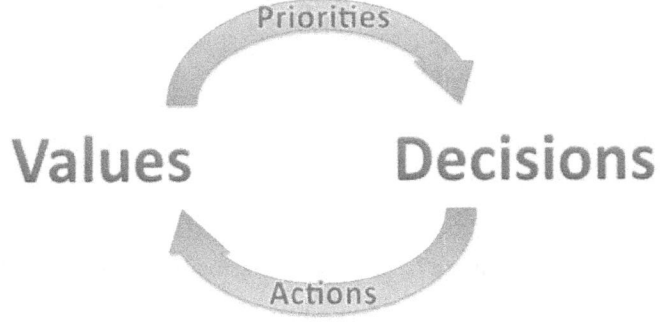

Figure 7.3. The Values Decisions Cycle

Keep the values cycle (Figure 7.3) in mind as I share the story of "David," who had a stroke before the age of fifty because, in his own words, he "cared too much about a bunch of people and a small company that did not care about me." Luckily for David, the stroke was not serious and he made a full recovery. But this brush with death gave him pause, and led him to reexamine his basic values.

Prior to the stroke, David had a company-first value system, meaning that he gave priority to things he thought could help the overall welfare of the company. For example, he'd "never leave work unfinished." So the moment it came time to take a break and head to the gym, he would decide to skip his workout to "catch up."

David's action created an example of cognitive dissonance, a conflict between the desire to be in shape and the desire to help the company. The psychology research has shown that people will find a way to reduce this mental conflict, and since the action in the past cannot be changed, one way to reduce the conflict is to elevate the importance of the path taken. In other words, staying on the computer reinforced the underlying value that the company comes first. As a result, in the future he would be more likely not only to skip the gym but do make other decisions that favored the company over people. And indeed, David missed his wedding anniversary, kids' birthdays, and he didn't go on a ski trip with friends because, he said, "The company needed me."

Although David recovered fully from the stroke, he was laid off less than a year later, which was a blow to his identity. "Maybe I don't have it anymore," he told me in a quiet voice. I knew exactly what he meant, because at one time the value I gave myself came from my job. And I also knew that if I hadn't changed my life a few years earlier, it could have been me with the stroke.

At first, the transition was hard for David. After the layoff, he was frantic to find another job. He trolled the Internet, considering jobs that weren't even in his field. He said to me, "What I really need to do is to close a few deals to get my confidence back." Again, I could relate because if I had been laid off a year earlier, I would have felt the same way. David quickly found another (suitable) position, which helped him get his confidence back and ease into the transition from company-first values to people-first values.

David was in a good marriage and had three children, a daughter in college and two boys in high school. David used this experience to change his life, and he reconnected with people-first values. In order of importance his priorities became:

1. Personal Health
2. Family
3. Work

It's not that work was unimportant to David; it just wasn't as important as his health or his family. And this translated directly into a different set of priorities and decisions. For example:

- He took a spontaneous trip to see his daughter at college, something he had never done before.
- He stopped working at five because he wanted to have time to cook and eat dinner with the family. Previously, he'd be on calls and email till eight and would get off the phone starving and crabby, usually running out to Burger King for dinner.

- When traveling to the corporate office, he made it a point to go to the gym instead of going early to the office with colleagues.

None of these changes are earthshaking in and of themselves, but together they arise from the same source--a shift in David's personal identity. Identity is one way that we translate our values into actions. Imagine this internal dialog: "What would a person who puts people first do, go into work early or go to the gym?"

After the stroke, David changed his values, and refocused his personal identity. He had been in the habit of deriving positive reinforcement from job-related activities. When David shifted his focus, he got positive reinforcement from the family related activities.

Change Habits to Change Idolatry

One reason people practice idolatry is habit—we just keep doing what we are used to doing. And habits can be hard to change. In his book, *The Power Of Habit*, Charles Duhigg explains that in a typical habit there is some kind of cue that triggers a routing behavior which in turn brings a reward.[76] (See Figure 7.4) For example, if someone puts a plate of cookies on the table in front of me, I will take and eat a cookie, even though I am trying to lose weight. The cue is the cookie, the behavior is eating, and the reward is a burst of pleasure and sugar. In addition, when my brain sees the cookies, it anticipates the pleasure, and I start craving the cookie, such that it becomes harder and harder not to take a cookie. This habit of eating cookies overrides my long-term desire to keep my weight under control.

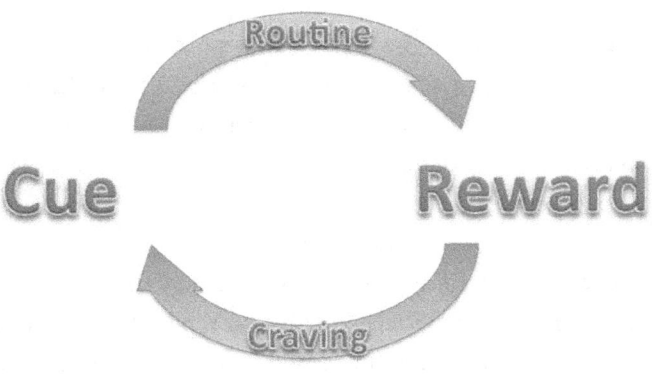

Figure 7.4 The Habit Loop[77]

Habits are mediated by a primitive part of the brain called the basal ganglia, which operates independently of rational, cognitive thought. In other words, a habit is similar to a reflex, something we just do without thinking. The best way to change a habit is to disrupt one of the three stages of a habit, which means avoid the cue, change the behavior, or change the reward.[78]

In David's case, the work stress became a self-fulfilling prophecy. For example, Duhigg explains that checking email becomes a habit. Executives get a reward from the temporary distraction a new email provides. For me, I got an adrenaline burst from all kinds of work-related issues, and I think that was David's issue as well. The rewards for his people first-values were calm and peace.

If you asked David before his stroke if it was healthy for someone to work 100 hours a week, I think he would have said,

"Of course it's unhealthy." But if you asked him if he was risking his health, I doubt he would have perceived himself at risk. This is one of those positive illusions we discussed in Chapter 5. People are not very good at evaluating themselves. For example, most people think they are above average drivers, and "twenty-five percent of people believe they are in the top one percent in their ability to get along with others."[79] Larry Holmes, the former heavyweight boxing champion was asked if he was concerned about injury during a comeback in his forties. His answer was telling: "You always think it will be the other guy who gets hurt, not you."

Overwork is an unrecognized danger that has significant health consequences. One in three Americans describe themselves as chronically overworked,[80] and thirty percent of Americans are chronically sleep deprived.[81] I won't bore you with a laundry list of statistics about the dangers of sleep deprivation and stress, in part because research suggests that statistics are not an effective way to change behavior. However, the "156 million visits to doctors' offices, clinics and hospital outpatient departments in 2005 [for mental health issues]"[82] suggest that we have an unrecognized epidemic on our hands. I wonder how many of these people were experiencing chronic stress but didn't think they were at risk for a health issue.

I will let you know why in general statistics have little impact on behavior: we are not of one mind. In other words, different parts of the brain mediate different types of behaviors. We already saw one example of this earlier in the chapter when we learned about habits and the basal ganglia. On a behavioral level, scholars like Plato and Freud have written about the different properties of the mind for thousands of years. The metaphor I like best is of a rider on an elephant.[83] The rider is the rational, conscious mind, and the elephant is the unconscious (emotional) mind. The rider can point the elephant in a certain direction, but if the elephant doesn't want to go, it won't.

At the end of the day, our emotions are in control. But that doesn't mean we can't change them. David's stroke was an emotional jolt that led to rapid life change—he recognized how precious life was and started to put people first. The moment I recognized my corporate idolatry gave me an analogous emotional kick, which led to steady changes in my life as well. And here's the really good news: you don't need to have a health crisis or a religious experience to change the elephant—a positive emotional carrot can be just as effective.

By reading this book, you have already begun the process of reorienting yourself towards people-first values. There can only be one top priority, and consciously deciding that people, yourself, your friends, and your family come before the company is a critical step on the path.

One Step You Can Do Today to Relieve Overwork

If you are overworked, stressed, feeling stuck and want a more fulfilling life, your elephant is hungry for change. So if the elephant—aka, your emotions—want to change, why are you stuck? There is an even stronger emotional component keeping you in place.

If you are hoping for dramatic change, it isn't going to happen unless there is a crisis. David's story is a perfect example of a health crisis leading to a change in lifestyle. But if you'd like to change before you have a stroke, or before you run screaming from the building, hope is the best answer. Hope is a powerful emotion that is an effective enabler of change. As I've written before, I went from working ninety hours a week to less than sixty hours a week in less than a year without changing jobs, and without anyone at work noticing. Here is a step by step to make similar changes in your life.

1. Remind yourself that you are the type of person who puts people first and the company second. As you make decisions, try not to think about the professional consequences of your actions—think only about what a person who puts people first would do.

2. Secure a goods night's sleep every night by stopping work two hours before bed time. My internal dialog went something like this. *My health is more important than work, so I will not check email or open my computer after 9:00 PM. I need seven hours of sleep.* Keep this rule no matter what. People at work will adjust, assuming they even notice. You will feel the difference of being more rested right away.

3. Try making people the priority in the moment. For example, if it is story time, or you are having a drink after work with a friend, don't answer your phone or listen to message voicemail you receive until you are alone. Imagine being on a date with someone who says, "It's my boss calling, but you are more important to me, so I'll listen to the message in the morning."

Think about your life and look for a clearly defined, specific change that you can make to put people first. A small change means an easy win. In my example above, I set a hard and fast rule that I would close my computer and turn off my phone at 9 PM. What is one rule that you could put in place that would prioritize people over the company? All you need to do is show the elephant that change is possible, and it will start to move on its own.

The Power Mom Executive Changes Her Identity

Many people I've met are like "Janet Wolf," caught between competing identities. Janet has a Ph.D. from Cal Tech in Chemical Engineering and worked after grad school for the Boston Consulting Group. Janet is one of the most relentlessly positive people you'll ever meet, and I was not surprised to hear that at the end of a long engagement the president of an electronics firm recruited her to become vice president of corporate planning.

Janet was very interested in the position, but was nervous because she was four weeks pregnant and "wanted to make a good impression." (And this was ten years before Marissa Mayer made it hip to be a pregnant executive.)[84] When she told the president, she was delighted to hear his response: "Congratulations, I don't care."

Janet went on to be what I think of as the "power working mom." At work I doubt people perceived her as a mom, yet she was able to remain involved in her kids' activities. I asked her how she manages to do both. In her words: "I've been crystal clear with each boss—I have kids. There will be days I need to leave early, or can't get here early. I got the work done and it was never a problem. I got to move around to bigger and better things."

Janet is a Wolf, someone who is concerned with both the success of the organization and the welfare of the people she works with. And like Harry Lobo, she found herself in a difficult political environment. Janet described it as "ten smart guys at the top" who seemed to think that everyone else was "dispensable."

Janet's last manager at that company had "no desire to spend any time on talent management. [His attitude was] 'Get it done or else you suck and get out of here.'" This was difficult for Janet to deal with, because her values put her priorities in a different place—developing people was the key to successful long-term success of the company. And her network, both professional and personal, was huge, which was critically important after an unexpected layoff. Janet's comments, which she shared with me a month after the layoff, illustrate how her identity quickly shifted.

"These people don't value me, but it doesn't mean that I'm not valued. Your identity is so tied up with a company and a role, but then you realize that you are above all that. It doesn't matter that you may or may not be affiliated with a company right now. It's been an interesting awakening for me to realize that I'll be okay. It took a week for me to [figure this out]. I got so many calls and emails from friends. Yes, I do want to do something exciting next, but it's okay if it takes a while."

And given the size of her network, it didn't surprise me that Janet soon had another position that she described to me as her "dream job."

Janet Wolf described how her identity before the layoff as wrapped up in the company. What does it mean to have an identity wrapped up in the company?

We all have multiple identities that apply in different situations. Corporate idolatry arises when the company-first identity becomes dominant. In the year I transitioned from working ninety hours a week to less than sixty hours a week, I was in a virtuous cycle—the more time I spent at home, the stronger my parent/ husband/friend identities became, which in turn made it easier for me to work even less. And as I got more sleep, I felt better, which in turn strengthened my health identity, which in turn made it easier for me to find time for the gym.

For Janet, the change in her primary identity was catalyzed by a change in her environment. Janet solidified her identity as a people-first person as opposed to a company-first person only after she was laid off from her job. It took some distance and time for reflection to make the change.

Some people have a natural ability to achieve Life Balance, and it starts with a secure people-first identity.

The Balanced Achiever

"Sebastian Tate" describes himself as an outlier in the business world, not because of his results, but because of his priorities.

"I never had the drive to be president or VP. I made that decision pretty early. [For me] work needed to be interesting. If I'm doing work I don't find interesting, I'll go look for another job. I've always made decent money, and I'm not an extravagant person, so I never felt like I needed to make a lot more money because I needed to have more stuff. If for whatever reason [work] gets out of balance because you get a shitty situation, I start looking for another job, to find a situation that works for me. I may be different than a number of people that you talk to, that want to be king of the universe. But that's why I'm still doing product management at fifty."

Sebastian is tall and wiry, with close-cropped hair and a slow, deliberate speaking style that can drive an East-coaster like me crazy at times. But he has that Buddhist calm that makes you want to listen. I asked Sebastian if he ever felt work-related guilt.

"Guilt is something that you impose upon yourself. You either accept it or reject it. I always found it pretty easy to reject it. If someone comes to me with a last minute request because they did a shitty ass job planning, and then try to make me feel guilty, it isn't going to happen. I don't know where I was when I learned it, but I learned to try to replace guilt with responsibility. It's a much healthier emotion."

As I talked to Sebastian, part of my mind went back to a conversation I had when I was a hotshot in my early thirties. I was in a camping store, and the man behind the clerk told me that he was in marketing for ten years. I was polite, but I'm embarrassed to admit that I really looked down on him. *What a loser,* I thought. *He couldn't cut it.* Of course now I get it. I'm on the other side of the fence, and some former colleagues view me as the weirdo who left the beloved asylum.

I asked Sebastian if he thought achievement is important. "Many people want the big job, to get ahead. But if they get there, they realize they can't enjoy it. They don't have any time and are being pulled away from their family. For some people, it's just the accomplishment. I do get satisfaction from achieving certain goals. But in my life I try to make those personal goals outside of work. For example, running ten marathons, or kayaking this river, climbing this mountain. I am proud of my accomplishments."

I think Sebastian is an exceptionally secure person. One Machiavellian executive told me to hire "insecure overachievers [because they] have to show they're valued, wanted, needed, and work is a way of doing that. That's the trap—when work represents your value as a person. Work is sort of a bald gage of success, which isn't that meaningful, but it can be perceived as [self worth]."

Sebastian does not have that vulnerability because he gets his validation outside of work. But thinking back to my reaction to the dude in the camping store, and my obsession with my web traffic as I was blogging this book, I still have some work to do.

Chapter 7 Questions and Tips

1. Make a list of the identities you hold. (e.g., father, daughter, executive, friend, worker-bee). Which identity is the strongest? In other words, when a conflict comes up (like a text message during dinner), which identity takes precedence? Are you the people-first person who ignores the text to focus on those around you, or are you the company-first executive who jumps up to answer?

2. Think about your life and look for an easy win, the smaller the better. What is one rule that you could put in place that would prioritize people over the company?

CHAPTER 8
Build Your Community

One morning at my first job, I had a terrible moment of panic as I scanned my identity card to enter the building. What if I lost my job? I would not be allowed to enter this building. I couldn't talk to all of these interesting people, and I couldn't work on all this great stuff. Aside from my wife, I couldn't think of any friends in California who weren't at the company. Where would I go? What would I do?

Fear of isolation is normal. A friend of mine told me that being unemployed was like prison, because there was nothing to do all day. And taking pride in your work is normal and healthy. In fact, Judaism teaches that work is sacred. As Rabbi Janet Marder preached on Rosh Hashanah in 2012:

"In the Jewish worldview, work is sacred—it is building and creating a partnership with God in the work of creation."[85] Rabbi Marder explained that two famous scholars in the second century "would purposely carry burdens on their shoulders into the Study House because they wanted to show their students that manual labor should be respected. This view of work set Judaism apart from other [idol-worshipping] philosophies prevalent in the ancient world. The Greeks and Romans looked down on work; freedom from work was a mark of status and privilege."[86]

It was not my passion for the job per say that was the problem, because doing work is a good thing. The issue was the absence of other things in my life. I was working so many hours that I had not build relationships with people in other parts of my life. Over the years, as my community outside of work got stronger, the fear of being alone subsided.

Why Work Can Never Be Community

I define a community as a group of people with a common interest who look out for each other. In his book *Bowling Alone* Harvard Professor Robert Putnam rigorously documents the decline of community in America. Putnam points to decreasing membership in organizations like the PTA and Shriners, as well as a decrease in the frequency of informal get-togethers like Sunday picnics.[87]

Why is this noteworthy? Current research suggests that one of the most important sources of happiness is community.[88] Humans are inherently social creatures; we like to belong and interact with other people. And with less community, there are fewer opportunities to connect, and therefore fewer opportunities to generate happiness.

The workplace can look and feel a lot like a community. We spend most of our waking hours at work. A good leader will try to pull employees together towards a common purpose and create a sense of esprit de corps. And just as a community takes care of its members, many companies provide extensive lifestyle benefits to employees, such as on-site medical, dental, dry cleaning, and of course the granddaddy of them all, the on-site gym.

Unfortunately, layoffs are a reality at most companies. I've been through multiple layoffs in my career, although only once was I let go. It was much harder when I was one of those left behind and not laid off. I felt like one of the walking dead, wandering the halls, mourning those who were no longer there.

The personal connections at work often feel like friendships, and sometimes they are. But sometimes they aren't.

"Giorgio Danza" learned that lesson the hard way. Giorgi has a hearty laugh that matches the intensity of his personality. Think Polo, panache, and perfect. His hair is dark brown, short, and immaculately styled. Giorgio's sunglasses are amazing, and never the same.

After college, Giorgi worked for the same company for eighteen years, ten as a laboratory technician and then eight in product management. I asked him if the company felt like his community.

"Oh God yes, absolutely. I prided myself on having great relationships with people, from shipping to manufacturing. I think people saw me as very knowledgeable, experienced, knew how [the] company worked, [and] how to get things done. I stepped in [to the company] as a kid, literally as a child, and didn't learn stuff about politics that maybe I would have learned better if I had life experience outside of the company. "

I asked Giorgi about the layoff. "It was devastating. I did not see it coming."

I spoke to a former colleague of Giorgi's who thought it was a "crock" that Giorgi was laid off. "Sometimes your name just ends up on a list." Unfortunately, Giorgi's did.

He was so depressed that he spent a few weeks catatonic on the couch. Many people called, telling Giorgi how wrong it was that he was let go. But a few people he was really close with did not. "That really messed me up, not to hear from these people who I respected and I thought respected me." Years later he found out that his former boss told the team not to call Giorgi, because he was "so upset." It is hard to know why the boss did that. Maybe he made a genuine mistake. Maybe he was being self-serving. Giorgio was well liked, and many people did call in spite of what his boss said.

Ten years later, Giorgi talks like someone who has come to grips with a great loss in his past. The pain is still not that far from the surface. I don't know Girogi well, but he seems like a really good person. He speaks warmly of his brother, his niece and nephew, his friends. It is easy to see how someone who can care so deeply for other people can form those attachments at work, especially when he worked at the same place for all those years.

I can relate, because if I had been laid off a year earlier, I would have been in his shoes—utterly crushed. I think one of the greatest benefits of "busting my corporate idol" was the mental freedom I found.

In my subsequent jobs, I never forgot that I could be let go at any time. I realized that I would never invest all of my money in one asset, and should not invest too many of my personal connections in one place either. It was just too risky. So, I focused my energy on building a community outside of the workplace.

Lack of diversification is inherently risky. Would you put all of your money in a single stock? Any financial advisor would say you are crazy to do so. Diversification is the key to a sound financial strategy. The same holds true of your connections to other people. If all of your connection eggs are in the basket of your current company, you are at risk. Market forces beyond your control can turn the most wonderful of workplaces into the stuff of nightmares.

If your time profile indicates the risk of corporate idolatry because you are working more than sixty hours a week, I suggest that some life diversification is in order. You may really like your job or boss, and feel guilty about saying no to the company. I felt guilty at first when I started saying no. And just saying no is really hard, and it can lead to a lot of stress.

As an alternative, find something to say yes to, an activity that you decide is a higher priority than the company. By making something else a higher priority, and making decisions day-to-day that allocate time to the alternate activity, you will start to work fewer hours as a matter of course. Here are a few suggestions to help you find something to say yes to:

1. Make a list of the things you liked to do when you were younger. Is there anything you'd like to start again?
2. Join a class that a friend is taking. At minimum you'll get more time with the friend, and you might find something new that you really like.
3. If someone invites you to something, say yes! Community opportunities can be as rare as career opportunities.
4. Put the new activity on the calendar—you will be far more likely to follow through if it is on your schedule.

It's not complicated, just scary and hard to begin. But once you start to connect with other people outside of work, you will feel a positive pull to keep on connecting.

First Align with Your Spouse

The changes I made in my life would have been much harder without the support of my wife. We planned my exit from the corporate world for two months, looking at the finances primarily, to see if we could pull things off with only her salary to live on.

What was key, however, was not the raw numbers per se, but our shared values.

We made it a priority to reduce the stress in our lives, and knew that if I were home life would be easier. Fewer late fees because we could more easily stay on top of things, and less scrambling every time the car broke or one of the kids got sick. If our priority had been getting a new BMW every two years, and expensive shoes every month, I would still be working to maximize our income.

It was amazing how much less money we spent after I became a stay-at-home dad. Off the top, we saved money on childcare, gardening, lunches, and dry cleaning. But we saved even more money on big-ticket items that we didn't really need. We'd be in Costco and buy something expensive on a lark. Looking back on it, I think these purchases were a palliative for stress.

And while not everyone has a family, as we shall see in as the chapter progresses, everyone has the ability to grow a community of people who share their values.

The Key to Reducing Chronic Overwork

Remember David from Chapter 7, whose stroke led him to recognize his corporate idolatry, and switch to a people-first identity? Family and community was an essential part of his change. David's wife was thrilled that he was more focused on the family and his health. And I was amazed to hear that David and his wife decided to sell their large house in an affluent, gated community for a smaller, but very nice home in a more rural area. It meant changing school districts with kids in high school, but everyone was on board, looking for a less stressful life together.

David seemed surprisingly relieved to move. He said it was very stressful to maintain what he called "the façade"— making sure "you acted a certain way." The kids needed expensive clothes; Sears was not allowed. (I didn't ask about Chez Target, my family favorite, but I strongly suspect it was also out of bounds.) But David's move wasn't about the materialism per se; it was the people in the community that made him uncomfortable. He told me that one parent he met wouldn't let her kids go to a certain person's house because of the brand of coat the kid was wearing.

David's de-emphasis on materialism was probably the most extreme example I encountered. (Of course David is also the only person I interviewed who had a stroke before the age of fifty, which gave him a particular urgency to change his life.) David also made changes that were less extreme, more typical for people looking to build a community. For example, he started going to the gym a few times a week *with his buddies*, which reinforced the identity change of making people a higher priority than his company.

Who we choose to associate with is the key to change. By analogy, an alcoholic cannot spend his or her free time hanging out in bars, even if they are only drinking soda. Eventually, the environment will lead to a relapse. Similarly, if you want to move to a lifestyle that is less work centric, it is critical to find people who share those values.

Building Community When Single

One question I have been asked is: Greg, I'm single. The suggestions to spend more time with family do not apply to me. I'm on my own, and my work is what I have. What can I do?

My answer can be found in the corporate idolatry time profile first presented in Chapter 7, (Figure 7.1). Working too many hours squeezes out the opportunity to do other things in life. Building a community is particularly important if you are single because we all need people to support our change in priorities.

The first step is to leave the office. "Louis," a Silicon Valley business development and strategy executive did just that. Louis was a chronic over worker, and started leaving the office early to give himself the opportunity to meet new people. Here is how he describes the experience.

"You never know what that [new person or thing will be], but you're not going to find him or her ... staring at your spreadsheet. Part of it is chance encounters, and so you are not going to create new parts of your life unless you have the opportunities to encounter new places or new foods or new people or people from your past. If you limit your chances of encountering those things, in a sense you only have yourself to blame. By spending the hours from 6:00 PM to 10:00 PM working on your spreadsheet, you are vastly limiting the hours where you can discover new things about yourself."

To start to build community, make a list of the different parts of your identity. What is your work identity? What is your home identity? Put at least three things on the list. Pick one or two to focus on. These should be identities that help you connect with other people. Are you a sports fan? Buy season tickets to the local football team with a friend. And do something for other people—offer to drive or to order the tickets. What habits and customs do you need to change, and what habits can you develop to start supporting the new identity?

One great thing to do is to set a time when you will leave every day. Better yet, schedule a class that will force you to get out of the office. I interviewed "Julie," a software marketer, who mentioned taking a dance class. I asked what got her started. She said, "I was frustrated at work and needed a reason to get out of there. I was doing dance four days a week."

When you leave work early for a fun activity, the other people attending *also* have made the decision not to work. These are the type of people you want to connect with. Julie met her husband on the dance floor.

I interviewed another marketer who joined a rowing club in his early thirties. He met his wife. Another executive I talked to was having trouble meeting people outside of his office. He joined eHarmony and met his wife there. He particularly liked eHarmony because it helped him meet someone who worked in a completely different field.

In each case, these people made a conscious choice to reach out to others within the context of things they liked to do. And in each case, they used this outside activity to cut back time spent in the office.

I can't claim to be a dating guru, but this much I know: no one ever got laid spending the evening with a spreadsheet.

The Danger of Mistaking Work for Community

Remember Sue from Chapter 6, the successful VP who was secretly battling migraines every morning, crying, and not wanting to go to work? Of course it didn't start that way.

"When I was more junior, [it] felt like we were going somewhere. There was financial success, bonuses, and I moved up quickly. I appreciated being recognized. It was an absolute pleasure. The team stuck together for four years and we liked each other. Many nights we'd go to the gym, come back, and stay till ten. We were willing to do that—it was fun."

In many ways, what Sue is describing is a community—people you like to be with who provide support and conquer obstacles together. When I asked her if it felt like community, Sue agreed. "I loved the company. Marketing got along with development and sales, and it felt like you were a part of something. The day in, day out conversations were positive. Everyone was working towards the same goal. It was fun." (As I wrote earlier in the book, a common sign of a positive work environment is the feeling that everyone was working together. We are social creatures—most people like that feeling.)

When the company started having trouble maintaining the high growth rate, things got ugly. "There was this one person—I thought it was friendship but she didn't hesitate to stab me in the back without a second thought." And that was not an isolated case. Sales, marketing, and development—departments that had worked so well together in the past—were now caught in a cycle of personal and political attacks. And then the layoffs began.

I think it was this sense of community that drove Sue to stick with it, to try to "be the one to bring it back." Her superhuman and futile efforts made her very sick. The body starts to malfunction after prolonged periods of stress.

A company isn't a real community; it just provides a community-like experience. You can never be kicked out of a real community, but a company can and should get rid of anyone if business conditions warrant it. I get really nervous when I read about these companies that provide everything from laundry to dental services. Getting everything on the company campus is inherently isolating and gives fewer and fewer opportunities to make connections outside of work. I have relationships with my dry cleaner, my doctor, and numerous baristas in the greater San Carlos area.

These little daily interactions make a difference in the long run. It is nice to see a friendly, familiar face. If all of those faces depend on your continued employment, it becomes a social trap.

The Secret to Leaving Work Early

In his book, *Happy: Simple Steps to get the most out of life*, Ian K. Smith argues that happy people have more close relationships, the kind of friendships that take time to build and maintain. According to Smith (who is quoting the research of Martin Seligman and others), "A strong social network is also associated with lower levels of stress and a longer life span."[89]

Smith advises that someone without a network of friends should "put themselves in a position to meet new people." Interestingly, this is exactly how Sue told me she started to get healthy again.

Sue told me her decision to make a change came on a business trip. Being out of the office helped her realize how badly she wanted to change. Free from the daily meetings that started at 7:00 AM and often went until 6:00 PM, she realized that her life did not have time for anything else, and she needed "to go out and get a breath of fresh air." Here is how Sue thought about the problem:

"I'm not a runner or biker and I needed something to do that I really enjoyed. I like to learn, but I didn't want to go back to school. I wanted to find something that would challenge me in a way that wasn't drowning like work. I started pottery ... [and] I started getting involved in my community, which is important to me."

But it was community theatre that really caught her passion. "I love to sing, and I eventually started voice lessons. I just leave work and go. There is one woman who I hang out with. We have become really close friends and I would never have met her in the tech industry."

When I was blogging the book, I shared Sue's story on the Harvard Business Review Group on LinkedIn, and it exploded with interest. I prefaced the story by asking a question: "Is it okay for a key stakeholder to leave work early?" I shared the post with the HRB group on LinkedIn, and the response was explosive. The 200+ comments were varied, but I've summarized the most common ones:

- A good leader creates an environment where things can run smoothly even when they aren't there.
- As long as you are reachable by phone, it's okay.
- Don't leave too often or other people will start leaving early too.
- Leave whenever you have to as long as work is getting done.
- The mental connection to work is more important than whether you are physically at the office or not.
- Some people don't feel they had the freedom to leave early even if they wanted to.

There are three issues when you consider leaving the office early:

1. Can you leave without the organization falling apart?

   The answer to this question needs to be yes. If it is no, either the organization is not well led, or it does not have the right people. What could happen in your absence? Will it impact the revenue number?

Will it hurt customers? Will it send anyone to jail, or create a flag for auditors? Unless the answer to any of these questions is yes, don't even worry about it and leave.

If you have answered no, are you being honest with yourself? As I explained in the last chapter, we are often under the illusion that our impact is more important than it actually is. It may also be that you have not sufficiently empowered your team to make decisions in your absence, or you have not communicated your plans sufficiently.

2. Can your ego survive if the organization doesn't fall apart in your absence?

   I hate to admit it, but once upon a time, for me the answer would have been no. As I wrote in Chapter 7, many people suffer from the illusion of control, a belief that we have a much bigger impact on the outcome than we actually do. And when there is trouble in other parts of our life, work can serve as a refuge.

3. When you leave the office, which is more important to you, the work or the people you are with?

   Let's say you have stepped out for an hour to have lunch with a friend or to coach soccer for a child. The phone rings. Let's assume that the reason for the call is "legitimate" and that you will add value to the business by answering it. Should you take the call or call back when you are finished with lunch/practice? For me, once I got a work call or email, there was no turning off the work thoughts. And then I was no longer present for the people around me. Remember that you also "add value" to the life of the person you are with. So ask yourself which is more important to you, the job or the person?

Creating Rituals for a People-First Life

The Harvard Business Review suggests that people who are overloaded by work should "create rituals—highly specific behaviors, done at precise times, that become automatic and no longer require conscious will or discipline. For example, go[ing] to bed at the same time every night [ensures that] you consistently get enough sleep even when you don't feel like it."[90]

As a baseball fan, I'm all over rituals. During the 2012 San Francisco Giants World Series run, I listened to the first two playoff games (losses) on the radio, and then I watched next three (wins) on TV. It was a bummer, because I was afraid to turn the radio on for the rest of the playoffs, lest the Giants start losing again. Unfortunate, because Jon Miller and the other local radio announcers are so much better than the various clowns broadcasting on TV. But what could I do? I didn't want The Giants to lose on my account, and thus my superstition led me to continue to watch on TV.

My silly-but-true example illustrates something important about human behavior: much of what we do is driven by emotion, not reason. And while my turning on the TV was not a ritual per say, rituals serve the same function. We get emotional comfort from the sameness of an activity.

Rituals are one of the ways that corporate culture is perpetuated. A primary example is the quarterly company meeting, when all employees gather to hear senior management go through a scorecard of performance, talk about what is coming up, and try to inspire employees for the future. Employees at dysfunctional companies sometimes refer to these as "Kool-Aid sessions," while companies like Google and Yahoo use weekly all hands meetings as a way to build a culture of transparency and trust among employees.[91]

This tip from Harvard Business Review is spot on—rituals are an effective way to lower stress and reinforce desirable behavior. However, I disagree with the overt suggestion to use rituals as a means to maintain a work-first mentality. We can cre rituals to support a people-first life.

Sebastian Tate, who we met in Chapter 7, uses the ritual of an annual camping trip to maintain a healthy work-life balance. As you may recall, Sebastian takes his career seriously, and always wants to work at an interesting company. "I would struggle working for a company doing cosmetic surgery just to get rid of wrinkles." For Sebastian, work is decidedly not his community, and over the years he has surrounded himself with people who share his values about the relative importance of work and the rest of life. And every August for the last twenty years, Sebastian and his buddies get together for a men-only camping weekend.

It started with friends he grew up with, and over time has "evolved to be group of people across different companies." Sebastian explained that "guys want to get together and be guys." Sure, they have beer and hike, but what I found particularly interesting were the intense discussions about life. And I think it was the natural setting that facilitated the intensity of the community feeling.

There is something about nature that is special. Somehow people have a biological affinity to become more relaxed and healthy in a natural setting than they do in an urban setting. Sound like an exaggeration? In 1984 Ulrich showed that patients with a window facing a park have a faster recovery from surgery than patients facing a wall.[92] Since then, numerous studies have shown that access to green space reduces stress, improves cognitive function, and strengthens the immune system.[93] And green areas with water seem to have a bit of an extra benefit.[94] Of course anyone who has been on vacation to Maui knows that an ocean view costs more than a mountain view, which is more expensive than a garden view. In this case, market-defined value matches what the science suggests are the most valuable traits for wellbeing.

Creating Rituals for Your Long-Term Happiness

One of the themes of this chapter is to recognize the power community has over how we behave. Community establishes hidden rules for behavior and provides a set of rituals and customs to support the behavioral norms. At work the rituals are things like the all hands company meetings, which take place on a quarterly or weekly basis. At home community rituals may be anything from a formal community, like a church, to the informal men-only camping trip.

Many corporate cultures have an implicit company-first value system, which I have argued throughout the book promotes a modern form of idolatry. As I explained in Chapter 7, the first step to escape a life of corporate idolatry is to develop those parts of your identity that put people and not the company first. However, the power of corporate culture can be so powerful that it takes a strong community outside of work to counter-balance its influence.

A relationship with a true community works in two directions; if you support the community, it will support you in return. A company relationship, on the other hand, is one way. While a few companies like Southwest Airlines have a no layoff policy, this should not be taken as a lifelong commitment—there is nothing to prevent layoffs in the future. People who worked at IBM in the early '80s could not have envisioned the wide scale layoffs and the loss of the generous pension plans in the early '90s.

I recommend a personal risk reduction strategy, to establish rituals that support a commitment to community outside the workplace. The first of these rituals, which I will cover in the next chapter, is a Sabbath, a day without work.

Chapter 8 Questions & Tips

1. How do your values align with the people in your life? If you are married, what are your spouse's values? Which is more important, a new car or having you around more?

2. What opportunities are there in your life for chance encounters that may lead to community building?

3. How can you demonstrate to someone close to you that they are more important than your job? Write down a few ideas right now. For example, leaving work early for a kid's event, or shutting off electronics during dinner.

4. Make the bedroom a sacred space, for nothing other than sleep and sex. No electronics allowed.

CHAPTER 9

Paint Your Environment

My junior year in college, I was rush chairman at my fraternity, which meant I was in charge of recruiting new members. There was this one guy who came by a few times and impressed some of my brothers with his coolness. Others, like me, thought he was an asshole. We were a small house and did not turn away people easily. We also didn't have any guys who liked to brag about cheating on their girlfriends, and I was not up for letting one in. This was the dark ages of the '80s, when we used an index card to track each "rushee." Every week I would hand out the cards to other brothers who had the job of inviting them over for events. One of my brothers really wanted to help with rush, but he was terrible on the phone. I gave him the asshole's card every week. And the asshole quietly disappeared.

I can't exactly say that my choices were the model of honest behavior, but I was living according to my values in an organization that may have chosen another path. I now realize I was using organizational savvy (a skill I seemed to have lost during my ten years in the academic world, and one I had to rediscover the hard way in the business world).

Leadership maven Marian Cook defines organizational savvy as "understanding the professional culture you are in and working with it—instead of against it—to achieve your goals. It is understanding that "office politics" is a reality to be dealt with, not ignored or even looked down upon. Whenever two humans get together, there are "politics" at play that affect your performance, the perception of your performance, and therefore your pay. It is the portfolio of competencies, approaches, and behaviors used to navigate your career and organization with success and integrity."[95]

Your company has a value system, more commonly called a corporate culture. And as I wrote in Chapter 6, unless you are the CEO and have carte blanche from the board to clean house, your chances of significantly changing that culture are close to zero. It can be dispiriting to feel that one has no control over the environment, which is why the illusion of control is so prevalent in the workplace. But there is a solution.

Holocaust Survivor Viktor Frankl wrote that "forces beyond your control can take away everything you possess except one thing, your freedom to choose how you will respond to the situation."[96] The lesson I take from Frankl is this: having no control is not the same as having no choices. And when you have secured your identity as a people-first person and built a community of like-minded people, you are ready to make choices that you could never have made when you were caught up in corporate idolatry.

If your personal values are in conflict with the overriding corporate culture, you have three options:

1. Change your values to match the corporate values. Remember, values are defined by how we act, not by what we aspire to. Going along to get along equates to accepting the values of the organization. I did plenty of this in my career, and wrapped my acceptance in rationalizations so that I didn't feel guilty. I don't recommend this option, because once your values are compromised, it becomes easier in the future to do the next thing and the next. This path widens the gap between the values you live by,

and your inner self, leads to overwork, ill health, and loneliness.

2. Leave the company. Few people entertain this as a short-term solution, and often stay in unhealthy cultures longer than one would expect. I am lucky that I had the economic freedom to change careers. The bills need to be paid, and leaving is not always feasible.

3. Use organizational savvy to force the organization to act in accordance with your values. In other words, use the methods of power politics, financial forecasting, and alliance building to minimize or prevent actions that go against your values.

What follows is the Business Case for Good, which demonstrates how to use a forecast to make the company do the right thing.

For example, in 1994 Massachusetts had a statewide referendum that would have required companies to reduce the amount of product packaging. I lived in Boston and there was a raging debate between the environmentalists and the business community. One side said that excess packaging is bad for the environment and costly to the public. The other side claimed that the costs of packaging reduction would be astronomical and cost jobs. The measure was defeated 65% to 35%.

Fast forward to today—many companies cannot reduce their packaging quickly enough. The difference is that today there is a financial return driving the process. Less packaging brings lower costs, a green brand, and in some cases more ease of use. If you can deliver a better product at a lower cost, why wouldn't the company do it?

Corporations are in business to make money, and it is very hard to argue that a company should make less money. It is far more effective to make a Business Case for Good.

If your company must decide between doing the right thing (A), or doing the wrong but less expensive thing (B), the worst thing you can do is to argue for "A" based on ethics. Instead, use your creativity to create a business case. For example, argue that A will differentiate your product in the market and allow the company to command a higher price. Or, argue that "B" will have higher support costs, or that it might expose the company to a legal risk.

Whatever you do, don't EVER mention an ethical justification for A, not even as a fourth bullet point. I've used a Business Case for Good on several occasions, and invariably someone else said, "Of course we should do A. It's the right thing to do." This is a test. If you agree, someone on the other side will use your agreement to bring the argument back to ethics, and you will lose. Instead, be savvy and say, "That should not be a factor in the decision—we need to do what is best for the company."

You want this to become a contest of who has the best numbers. If you present better numbers than the other side, your company will start doing the right thing in spite of itself.

What Happens If Features Are Dropped For Launch?

Ever been on a project that is under time pressure to make a launch date? One common solution is to drop features from the product. For example, when Apple launched the iPad mini in November 2012, it did not have the retina display. I have no knowledge of how that decision was made, but I can easily speculate that this feature was not included to bring in the launch date.

"Sabina" was a product manager who had to make that very choice. She was managing on a new technology to accelerate scientific research. When the original product was scoped, it was designed to meet a set of unmet customer needs, and she created a healthy revenue forecast to justify the expense of development. Sabina explained the difficulty of creating a forecast for a new technology.

"When you build [mathematical] models, you try to make an intelligent metric," which was based on sizing the market and estimating the market share based on what the product could do relative to the competition. Sabina explained that she felt pressure to show significant value in doing the project, a positive Net Present Value (NPV). "I never felt that I wasn't being truthful, [but] with a brand new technology, it's sticking your finger in the air and making the best guess you can. There was equal pressure from myself and others."

A forecast is built on assumptions. One key (although often unstated) assumption is that the product will meet the customer's needs. Notice how the impact of the assumptions as Sabina continues her story.

"When I did the original model [at the start of the project], there were assumptions of what we could commercialize. [As the project progressed,] we had to cut out two-thirds of the features. … At that point if I had cut [the revenue] as much as I should have, the project may have been killed. Yet I believed in it enough for the longer term, not just first release." Sabina made a quiet internal assumption that it would take multiple iterations to get it where the customers really needed it to be.

Unfortunately, the organization was tied to the forecasts, and the actual revenue came in at 25% of the pre-launch levels. This in turn meant that additional development resources were not allocated to help the product grow. And life was difficult for Sabina, with lots of questions from her management team. "I felt like a failure because [the forecast] was so off."

I understand where she is coming from. I have twice managed a product that was selling below the forecast. The first time I felt terrible, but the second time I was only annoyed. The difference? By the second time I had busted my corporate idol, meaning that my personal identity was not longer tied up with the company. I was clear in my mind that the most important things to me were my health and the people in my life. And I had a strong community that I knew would be there for me whatever happened at work. Together, this gave me freedom to make different choices when "stuff happens" at work.

Let's revisit Sabina's situation and look through the lens of corporate idolatry to see what she might have done differently. As I wrote at the end of Chapter 3, corporate idolatry is driven by people, circumstances, and corporate culture.

People: Sabina's management supported her both publicly and, as far as she knows, privately. She did have a bit of a red flag when she first developed the forecast—her manager didn't ask any questions, and she felt a bit like she was out on a limb.

Circumstances: There were a number of challenging issues that Sabina needed to manage.

1. The company had previously licensed an expensive technology to develop the product. Thus she inherited "sunk costs" that made it harder to get a positive NPV.

2. Sabina was introducing a disruptive technology, which means an inherently slow uptake in the market, and more uncertainty about the time it will take to adopt.
3. Many of the dropped features would have brought ease of use and flexibility to the customers. What remained was a product good enough to prove that the technology worked to early adopters, but the sales potential was inherently limited without further development.

Culture: Sabina had reservations about the company culture. It was a big company with many products. The politics were getting more personal and nasty, and it seemed to her that the people who were doing well were brown nosers. And she personally knew several long-term sales reps who were put on a performance development plan (PDP) after one bad quarter. If they failed the PDP, the company could let them go without a severance package.

So stepping back, Sabina was in a cutthroat and unforgiving culture. Is it any wonder that Sabina's management was unsupportive of a new technology that was selling way below forecast? Sabina was too close to the company, and too worried that the project would be canceled to look at the situation objectively.

If Sabina had felt secure in a people-first identity, with the support of community outside of the workplace, it would have been easier to take on the difficult culture. And, it would have been easier for her to slash the revenue forecast when the features were cut.

How would the company have reacted? Maybe the project would have been canceled as she feared, or maybe the company would have accepted the lower forecast and the need for future investment. In either case, the situation would have been less stressful than the slow withering on the vine that comes from the stigma of an underperforming product.

Could she have been risking her career by speaking out? Maybe, but unless she was willing to take part in the prevalent brown nosing, her career advancement was probably limited at that company anyway. Today Sabina happily works at another company where she can speak her mind without fear of repercussions.

A Forecast is not a Prediction

You might be wondering what this has to do with your quest for a more balanced life. There is a right and wrong way to use forecasts. Forecasts are a good way of charting *possible* outcomes, such as whether a new product has the *potential* to be big seller. The actual outcome, however, can't be predicted, which is why every company should have a diversified portfolio of high risk and safer projects. (And why a one-trick pony startup is inherently risky.) But even if they have the proper portfolio mix, many companies, like Sabina's, act as if the forecast is a real prediction of the future.

Companies with too much emphasis on forecasting and making the numbers have a higher risk of an idolatry prone culture, which devalues people as individuals. And Sabina allowed forecasting to have too large an impact on her self-esteem.

Someone looking for balance in a numbers-first environment has a few options.

1. Play the politics to gain the power to set your own boundaries.

2. Take a lower profile product or project that will bring lower stress.

3. Become an expert at sandbagging the forecast.

Another option is to find another company with a different, longer term, and more flexible approach to doing business.

The People-First Corporation

I have explained how a "numbers-first" corporate culture is more likely to lead to corporate idolatry. There are also corporate cultures that are less likely to contribute to corporate idolatry. One of them derives from a fundamental way that a corporation is structured.

Remember from Chapter 3 that corporations are established by law? Under the standard legal framework, company officers and employees have a fiduciary duty to maximize shareholder value, and may actually be prohibited from taking wider social concerns into account when making decisions if shareholder value is negatively impacted.

For example, it is widely perceived that the formerly socially progressive Ben & Jerry's Ice Cream Company was forced to sell to Unilever, a large multi-national company, because it was in the best interest of shareholders. A close review of this decision debunks the myth that the company was legally required to sell to the highest bidder even though the founders did not want to sell.[97] But whatever the actual legal status, this perceived fiduciary duty is an argument that can thwart attempts to "do the right thing."

The Benefit Corporation (B Corporation) is a new type of corporation designed to get around this issue. According to Bcorporation.net, "Current corporate law makes it difficult for businesses to take employee, community, and environmental interests into consideration when making decisions." The B Corporation provides a legal framework to allow the creation of an organization that has a wider social mission beyond profit alone. In other words, the founding charter of a B Corporation includes a material benefit to society as one of its goals.

According to Andrew Kassoy, one of the leaders of the B Corporation movement, "Increasingly there are businesses that want to create value for all their stakeholders, not just their shareholders."[98] So by its very nature, a B Corporation will tend to attract people who care more about than just the bottom line. This type of environment is much more likely to be friendly to a balanced lifestyle. For example, on Glassdoor.com, a website with anonymous reviews of companies, Patagonia, a B Corporation, is highly rated both overall and for work-life balance.

Will a legal structure solve the problem of corporate idolatry? Not completely, but a B Corporation could be part of your answer, because it removes an obstacle to people-first values in the workplace. There is now an answer to the "we have a fiduciary duty to shareholders" argument, which is yes, but we also have a duty to meet our societal mission. I would not rely on this to ensure people-first behavior, but when combined with a good business case, it can make all the difference.

How to Redefine "What Is Best for the Company.

Throughout the book, I've argued that doing what is best for the company instead of doing what is best is a symptom of corporate idolatry. But to play devil's advocate, isn't doing what is best for the company what I was being paid to do at my job? Of course it was, but when someone feels the need to remind everyone of that, it often becomes an excuse to cover up the real motive. (The movie *Office Space* hits the ball out of the park on this topic. When the consultants Bob and Bob are brought in to lay people off, the first thing they do is to hang a banner that says, "Is this good for the company?")

I asked both Janet Wolf and Harry T. Lobo, two leaders I admire, what they thought about doing what is best for the company. They independently pointed out to me that what's best for the company is highly subjective. Harry was adamant that it was his job to do the best for the company, BUT he focuses on what is best *in the long term*. Will this decision build long-term value and long-term relationships with customers, or are we sacrificing the long term to meet short-term goals?

Harry told me that one of the things he found difficult in his time at the toxic culture was the incredible pressure at the end of the quarter, when "sixty percent of revenue came in the last forty-eight hours." The sales team was incentivized to do crazy deals to pull business forward, which in the short run helped maintain the stock price. In Harry's opinion, this built a "house of cards" because it was that much harder to make the number the following quarter.

Janet "Power Mom" Wolf told me of a situation where site closures were explained to the remaining employees as a positive step because they brought various product development teams together in house. Closer coordination would bring products to market more quickly, and thus better serve customers. Janet had visibility to the decision making process, and she thought the layoff was more about cost savings, combined with an arrogance that the closing sites (brought in by acquisition) were not as good. Janet told me that executives made comments like, "What do those people do all day?"

Janet did not think the loss of personnel and expertise would benefit the company in the long run. The company did not offer any relocation packages, which in Janet's opinion "spoke volumes" about what the executives thought of the people.

The lesson is that even in a toxic culture, there are leaders who define "the good of the company" in terms of the long-term interest and who value people. The trick is to find these leaders, and the pockets of relative calm and sanity they can provide. For example, Janet talked about how she tried to shield her team from the buffeting from the top. "What I found myself doing is I tend to be the shield. I've run several groups in my career. I'm transparent and share what can be shared, and I give perspective. I encourage them, something I don't get from my superiors."

When I was caught up in my corporate idolatry, I never considered certain positions because the products were not cool or not important enough. But as work became less important to me, I became more open-minded, and was delighted to get a job out of the limelight. There was less stress, and I had the bandwidth to focus on health and family.

What is the take home lesson? If you feel stuck in a difficult situation at work, changing the overall company culture is not a realistic goal. But, there may be pockets of relative calm within the company. If you don't want to leave the company, look for a team with different leadership.

ROWE Your Way to a Balanced Life

It really *isn't* the same everywhere.

As I have argued throughout the book, some company cultures tend to drive people towards unethical decisions.[99] In an analogous way, some company cultures drive people towards corporate idolatry. In companies with a culture prone to idolatry, employees are expected to "do what it takes" to meet deadlines, and to sacrifice their personal time if the boss asks. There are also companies with a lower idolatry risk. For example, companies that have adopted a Results Oriented Work Environment (ROWE) are in this class.

ROWE was developed by Cali Ressler and Jody Thompson when they were in the HR department at Best Buy. The philosophy behind ROWE is simple: employees are responsible for results. How they get there is completely up to them. Employees are given the freedom to decide when to come into the office and how best to meet their objectives. Daniel Pink argues that ROWE is effective because it provides employees autonomy, that is, control over their environment, which is intrinsically motivating.[100] This testimonial from an employee at the GAP, a ROWE company, seems to support that notion. "ROWE has been such a huge support and peace of mind. It allows me to not feel guilty when I need to take care of personal issues. I always meet my deadlines and find alternate time to complete my work." [101]

In general, I am skeptical about an individual's ability to change a company culture. However, Ressler and Thompson present a way to make it possible, with a website filled with business cases and slide deck templates to help you make the case for ROWE at your company.

The retailer GAP Outlet saw business productivity, employee retention, and employee satisfaction all measurably improve, based on metrics measured before and after the ROWE implementation.[102]

When I wrote about ROWE on Idolbuster.com, a full-fledged argument broke out in the comments section. "George" wrote,

"One of the main problems with ROWE is that everything needs to be quantified. All activities everywhere by everyone have to be defined in terms of measurable deliverables and set deadlines. (Otherwise, it is only rational for less supervised people to do less work and allow general expectations of productivity to slow forever.) [ROWE requires] a whole second overhead of having to track/manage/supervise the on time delivery of goals, which were probably impossible to set accurately in advance unless your work is highly predictable and routine (unlikely nowadays)."

George is representing the control mindset present in many companies, where employees are not respected, and are treated like children needing constant supervision.

"Ronnie," the CEO of Suntell, responded. (Suntell sells loan risk management software to banks and adopted a ROWE strategy a few years ago.)[103]

"We do NOT spend our time hashing out every nth detail or even supervising those details—if the time was spent on those benign activities, when would any results actually be met? What do those activities have to do with delighting the customer? "We give our employees complete freedom to meet a set of well-defined desired results—all of which come back to DELIGHT the CUSTOMER.

"There are some employees which I personally HAVE NOT SEEN since we migrated to ROWE. Do they meet results? Absolutely—actually even more so than when I beat them into submission and chained them to their desks in our old traditional (archaic) work environment!" Ronnie shared many specific financial metrics showing the financial success her company achieved in the two years after adopting the ROWE strategy. For example, revenue was up 185% while expenses decreased 12% and the customer retention rate more than doubled.

"So if you're not interested in results or delighting your customers or stakeholders," Ronnie continued, "I would certainly agree that you should continue to keep your employees under your patriarchal thumb and make damned certain you can see them at all times—that way you will feel comfortable and secure in knowing results being met. Plus, it justifies your position—after all, someone has to mind the children during the day."

My take home is that George is caught up in the idolatry mindset that the company needs to constantly exert control over its employees. Meanwhile Ronnie is showing that giving employees control over their time is good for business.

Don't Let Perception Overshadow Your Productivity

The last company I worked for had a thing about slackers. In a performance review, my manager told me that I got more done than anyone he had ever met. Five minutes later, I was told that my career could be slowed because I was perceived as a 9-to-5er. Huh? I'm irked to this day. Clearly results were not as important as perception.

This was a cultural issue—there was a regular review process that evaluated people in two dimensions—the quality of work and suitability for promotion. In practice, the second dimension was a proxy for who showed up the most. Yes, I left at 5:30, but why did that matter when I was getting so much done?

In hindsight, I made too big a deal out of my life outside of work. For example, I always told my manager whatever kid activity I had done the previous weekend, and let him know that I would be leaving work early once a week to coach soccer at 3:30. He told me that I had trained him not to expect an answer to his Saturday emails until Monday morning; he admitted that he was surprised that he was okay with that. Yet in spite of my productivity, the company had me in the "not committed" column.

My only regret is what I said, not what I did. My highest priority was time outside of work. I forgot a fundamental rule about the workplace: every time you open your mouth you are broadcasting a perception about yourself. I should have talked less about the kids and more about what interested my manager—how hard I was working to make the numbers.

Learn How to Say No to Meetings

As you shift your priorities to people and start to work fewer hours, there will come a point when someone pushes you to do more. There is always more work to do, and if you don't set firm boundaries around your work, no one else will. As Jody Thompson, champion of ROWE, said on YouTube, what is the point of getting your work done early if it only means that you will be given more work?[104]

Even if the corporate culture is nowhere near adopting ROWE, you may be able to negotiate with your manager for more flexibility. The key is the first two words of the acronym—Results Only. What results do you need to deliver to have the most impact on your organization?

To figure this out, write a list of everything you are working on and the put them in rank order. I used a list like this to negotiate priorities with my manager. I explained why I thought certain things would have a larger impact. Usually he agreed, but occasionally we decided to change the order. And when he later asked me to do something that took a lot of time but wasn't in the top three, I would say, "Yes I can do it, but it will mean that X deliverable will be pushed out a few days. Is that okay, or would you prefer me to wait on the latest thing that you need?"

Next, I declined meetings that weren't in the top three, especially last minute or "one off" requests. They add up to a lot of time during the week, and those extra hours take away from time at home. Sometimes it was hard, because other parts of the company thought I should be helping them, especially sales. But I held firm if taking the meeting meant working at night. (And sometimes I adjusted priorities to make sales support a top three.)

As a product manager, I was constantly inundated with requests from many different directions. A priority list gave me the power to say, "I'd love to help, but my manager has told me that A, B, and C are higher priorities." I tried to be sympathetic when I said no, and whenever possible I offered alternatives, such as a website to find information, a promise to make time at a specific point in the future, or I delegated to someone else.

I always made sure I delivered high quality, on-time work for the top priorities. It was in effect a contract I had made with the manager. I was given more flexibility in return for higher quality, more impactful work. I needed to hold up my end of the deal.

There will be times when your manager asks you to drop everything and put something together for him at the last minute. When that happens, don't be afraid to delay another deliverable, with a quick note to the appropriate stakeholder(s) explaining why it will be late. I found that transparency is respected by others, and it helps build allies, even when saying no. If the other party insisted that I help, I let the two managers duke it out over what is a higher priority.

Your manager may not like owning the responsibility of the trade off, especially if you have a history of working weekends and staying late to deliver last minute, "urgent" requests. BUT, limiting how many hours you work will make you much more effective and a greater asset to your manager and the company. And if your manager doesn't recognize this, pull out some data.

The Impact of Sleep Deprivation

When we work too many hours, we don't get enough sleep. According to the National Health Interview Survey conducted from 2005 – 2007, 30% of Americans get less than six hours of sleep per night.[105] On a personal level, sleep deprivation leads to higher rates of traffic accidents and some serious health issues like high blood pressure and diabetes. In short, being tired is bad for you.

James Maas, my Psych 101 professor at Cornell, studies sleep deprivation. His website summarizes it well: "Recent medical research proves that sleep deprivation literally makes you stupid, clumsy, stressed out, unhealthy and will shorten your life."[106]

I spent plenty of time sleep deprived, and it didn't feel that bad to me. And the latest research explains why. Brain imaging studies comparing rested and sleep-deprived people have shown that "individuals who are sleep-deprived experience periods of near-normal brain function, but these periods are interspersed with severe drops in attention and visual processing. ... The periods of apparently normal functioning could give a false sense of competency and security."

Aside from the research, let's step back and think about it. Can you do your best work if you are tired or sick? Can you effectively lead a team if you are stressed out? Without recovery time, can you be creative and sharp? Does a big fight at home with your spouse help or hurt your work?

And on the positive side, are you happier going to work Monday morning if you had a hot date the previous weekend? How many hot dates happen when you work all weekend?

I doubt that whether you got laid or slept well would even be considered by your manager as something that impacts workplace results. But what if you could get more done if you worked fewer hours, and can prove it? It can be done, if you can conquer the fears that keep you from even trying. I know because I've done it.

When having the conversation with your manager about shutting down in time to get a good night's sleep, remember to make a business case, not a personal request. Even the Wall Street Journal admits that "a good night's rest is good for business." For example, "Harvard scientists estimated in 2011 that sleep deprivation costs U.S. companies $63.2 billion in lost productivity per year." [107] Tired people make mistakes.

As you prepare to have "the conversation" with your manager, first think about what motivates them: Are they a Scorpion, a Fox, or a Wolf? Your pitch depends on the answer. Remember:

- A Fox is motivated purely by self-interest, so be sure to emphasize how being rested will help you help him.

- A Wolf is motivated by what is best for the team/company. Emphasize how much more productive you will be, and how you will be a better teammate and manager.

- A Scorpion is motivated by a personal worldview and vision. These are the managers with tunnel vision, with a single minded focus on doing what they think is right, even if it is self-defeating. (Steve Jobs is a very famous Scorpion.) Explain to the Scorpion how focusing on the top three priorities, and having time to recharge at night will allow you to be more effective doing [insert the Scorpion's mission here].

This type of priority and boundary setting may be very unusual at your company, which is why you will need all of your savvy skills to make it happen. And be sure to emphasize that the work will get done, and that by getting more rest you will become more effective and efficient. Coming to work as your best self can only help the company. You may be labeled as a 9-to-5er as I was, but so what? I was incredibly effective, and they never would have gotten rid of me. Did this slow down my advancement? Maybe, but again, so what? Advancement was not as important to me as a balanced life. Remember the overarching goal is to put people first in your life, which means the company can take a lower priority.

And if your boss still says no, in spite of the empirical and scientific evidence that a balanced life makes a better employee? Well then you know where you stand, and how important you really are to the company. See if he will give it a try for a week or two as a pilot. If he still says no, I would document the conversation with your manager to give you legal protection, and stop working at 9:00 PM anyway. And, I would probably start looking for a new job.

Why You Should Play Politics

Earlier in the chapter, I shared how I was productive but perceived as "not committed" at my last job before I left the corporate world. In a way they were right; the company was not the most important thing in my life. But I was committed to producing high quality, professional work. Frankly, I would have stayed longer if I had been promoted.

I'm happy with how things have turned out, but sometimes I wonder if I should have been more like Sheryl Sandberg, COO at Facebook, who used to hide her 5:30 departure to take care of the kids.[108] I wanted to make a statement, and went out of my way to let everyone know that after-hours was out of bounds.

To navigate office politics successfully, there are a couple of things you should keep in mind.

Successful upward management requires firm boundaries and clear communication. For example, I did not answer emails in the evening. I didn't ask permission not to answer, I just didn't. My manager once told me how he learned not to expect a response from me to weekend emails until Monday morning, and he was surprised that he was okay with it. Here is a little secret—I did check email once a day on the weekend, but I did not answer because it never was an urgent issue. I trained everyone not to expect an answer, and they stopped sending me emails. When the workday started, I was sure to get to my most important email right away, sometimes by phone or an in person visit to the manager's desk. By my actions, I was signaling my work boundaries while paying attention to what my manager needed.

Poor upward management came when I got arrogant. I told my manager my strategy, how I deliberately trained him not to expect email from me. It pissed him off, and rightly so. I was showing off, and I think my arrogance held back my career in an unnecessary way. I had what I wanted: a life that put people first, and I was no longer caught up in corporate idolatry. I didn't need to rub his nose in it. I think my desire to champion workplace flexibility was a holdover from an earlier time in my career, when I thought that I was above politics.

You Are Not above Politics

When I first entered the corporate world, I was under the illusion that I was above politics. I did excellent work and thought that data and passion for the customer would carry the day. I explained my philosophy to a new mentor over lunch, at a time when I was looking for answers to my crazy life. I think my exact words ended with "I don't play politics because I don't need to."

He laughed. "Okay," he said after taking a sip of coffee. "You may think that, but I assure you that others in the organization don't think that way."

Boy was he right.

If you've made it this far through the book, you probably realize that I've grown up quite a bit since then. On some level, I knew about the people who I now call Foxes, manipulators only out for themselves. But I failed to recognize that sometimes a Fox has power, and makes getting more power a priority. Like many others, I viewed politics as inherently manipulative and therefore bad.[109]

Eventually, I woke up to the reality that politics exist in every company and impact every person. In good companies, politics revolve around competition between groups for resources, or differing views on business strategy. In unhealthy companies, politics are about ego, empire building, and it gets very personal.

By not playing politics I was abdicating some of my power, and thus unable to effectively do my job or set boundaries around my home life. And I was severely under-gunned when I was attacked by a powerful Fox. Politics is a tool, and like any tool it can be used for good or ill.

Harvard Business Review authors Kent Lineback and Linda Hill champion using politics for good purposes, arguing that politics is about building a network of people you can count on, people who work together for common cause and for mutual benefit. Lineback and Hill write that people who don't play politics associate mainly with friends at work, and therefore don't have access to information and allies that will help navigate the political currents, whatever they may be.[110]

Lineback and Hill wrote a series of great tips for building a network in their HBR article "Stop Avoiding Office Politics."[111] Here are two that I particularly like:

- "Work with others for *mutual* advantage, not just your own." I would add that *mutual* advantage also means there is something in the exchange for you too. Doing favors for someone without expecting anything in return *at work* is not a way to build a network, it is the way to become a doormat. There are just too many people who will take advantage of people willing to pick up the slack. Remember the Rule of Self-Preservation from Chapter 2: if you don't take care of yourself, no one else will.

- "Build ongoing, productive relationships with *everyone* you need to do your work, as well as those who need you, not just those you like." This means that you may need to work with scumbags, assholes, eggheads, or airheads that you normally would prefer to avoid.

If you are like me, someone who isn't a natural politician, beginning to engage others may seem a bit daunting. My suggestion: try one new thing, like inviting someone to lunch who works in another department. It will build your network, and you'll enjoy having a fresh face to talk to. As you get to know them, listen for a way you can help them. Offer to help, and when they thank you, be sure to say, "I'm sure you'd do the same thing for me."

But be careful and take it slow. If you try to become an overnight Machiavelli, you are likely to get squashed by the professional players in the game. But little by little, you can start to acquire some chits that can blunt the influence of the bad actors. What you want are people who are in your corner and who will tip you off if someone is acting behind your back.

If you are more junior, it may be hard to identify the movers and shakers in the stratosphere of the company. The advice is the same: get to know other people outside of your local area, and over time you'll find the real influencers.

If you choose to stay in the corporate world, politics are a reality. As Plato said, "One of the penalties for refusing to participate in politics is that you end up being governed by your inferiors." On the flip side, if you choose to leave the corporate world, you'll still have to deal with politics. During my time as a stay-at-home dad, I had to deal with politics over how to coach a soccer team of nine-year-old girls. It was crazy, but where there are people there will be politics.

Most of what happens in a company is beyond your control. But with the support of people outside of work, you will be strong enough to surf the waves that will push you to work longer hours, or make decisions that conflict with your values. And with a network of allies at work, you will be better positioned to resist those pushes directly.

In the last and final chapter, we'll explore what life looks life after you've busted your corporate idol.

Chapter 9 Questions & Tips

1. What are the values of your company? If it were a B Corporation, do you think it would make a difference?

2. What are the levers of power that you have access to? Examples include the revenue forecast, performance data, and the customer complaints database. How can you use those resources to construct a Business Case for Good?

3. How far will your company go to make the numbers? Where do the numbers come from? If you can't control the forecast, what can you control?

4. Who are the leaders in your company who seem to focus on the long term? Have you ever considered working for them? Is there a department that in the past seemed too boring that you would consider working for because they have a people-first leader?

5. Make a list of people in other departments, and start inviting them to lunch.

CHAPTER 10
The Balanced Life

Here I was, writing a book that advocates family over work, when I canceled our annual President's Day ski week vacation to attend the 2012 San Francisco Writer's Conference. I felt bad about doing it, especially because we were going on vacation with another family. But simplistic slogans like "family over work" are just another face of idolatry. Life is complicated, and sometimes there will be times when we decide to honor our career goals.

The word "canceled" comes from my inner voice of guilt and doubt. The reality is that I made the decision with the full support of my wife and friends, who understood how much the conference could help get the book out. And with five months notice, we found another time to ski, although it cost us a bit more.

A year later, I was faced with the same choice—The San Francisco Writer's Conference always falls on Presidents Day Weekend. In 2013, I picked the ski trip, even though from a career standpoint, I "needed" the conference even more that year, to help me self-publish. And I was sad that I wouldn't get to spend time with so many other writers.

Looking back on my blog posts from that time, the fear that I was missing a "make or break event" was very real. At the same time, the rational part of my brain reminded me that the "make or break" feeling was just an illusion. Now, I hardly remember the conflict, but I do remember a great time skiing!

Life Is Better, but Challenges Remain

To give you a preview of the post-idolatry world, I no longer worry about money. Okay, truth be told, I never really worried about money. I grew up poor and have always felt that I could get by with less.

But when I was making money, I sure spent a lot of it. Part of the reason I spent money was that I was stressed. I needed that fancy dinner to forget the office, and as a visible reward for the hard work. And I tended to make big impulse buys. Like art. My late uncle always used to say that your standard of living would rise to meet your income. He was right. And the reverse is also true. As the stress went down, my spending went down too.

Before I resigned from my job three and a half years ago, my wife and I spent two months examining our finances. She is so much better at budgeting than I am, and was quickly able to pull together the numbers. Where could we cut back if we lived on one income, not two? It was amazing how much money we could save without depriving ourselves. Like I mentioned earlier, we saved money on after-school babysitting, dry cleaning, commuting expenses, library fines, and un-submitted insurance reimbursements. And because I was cooking, we saved money by not eating out. Our tax bill decreased too.

There is one other aspect of working fewer hours—it may save your marriage. While this didn't come up in the interviews, I meet people on a regular basis here in Silicon Valley who filed for divorce because their spouse was working all the time. Or, someone comes home early from work and finds their spouse in bed with the proverbial mailman. A divorce will cost you plenty, and if you aren't willing to put the time into the relationship, you may be in for a terrible surprise.

As I wrote in the last chapter, it is impossible to predict the future. But there is one question that I think everyone should be able to answer: if you lost or quit your job tomorrow, how long could you live comfortably without earning any money?

As you conduct the exercise, assume your burn rate will be the same. It will almost certainly go down, but the purpose here is to understand where you stand without becoming anxious that your life will need to radically change. You may be more secure than you realize.

If you have only one month of savings in the bank, it is time to reduce your spending immediately and start to save. If you can live for at least twelve months without income, as I could, there is less reason to be afraid. In this case the real fear isn't over money per say. It is a fear of deprivation, the fear that you will have to give up things that you like. In fact, rich people fear poverty far more than poor people. Don't let the fear rule you.

Here is a story from "Brian," a Silicon Valley executive who got 150 emails a day when I first interviewed him. He accumulated over 1,000 unread emails every month. Brian had grown accustomed to working in somewhat chaotic environments. Here is how he describes his finances.

"I don't like living my life with any financial uncertainty. I have a very clear financial situation that I have become accustomed to. I have a certain lifestyle I lead. It's not like I spend money lavishly, but I like to go on nice vacations, and I like being able to buy the things I want. For example, if I'm in Sports Authority and I see something I want, I'm going to buy it. I was there for something else, and there was a driver on sale. I didn't need a new driver, but it was like half price and last year's model."

Since the interview, Brian changed jobs twice, both because of layoffs. In other words, he stayed with the chaotic jobs for fear of putting his finances at risk, and ended up without a job anyway. There is no such thing as financial certainty in this world, so why not try to have a life you'll enjoy?

My advice is to focus on the life you'd like to lead, rather than on having less money. Do you want a job with fewer emails? Fewer emails will mean less pressure to work at home, which in turn opens time for family and friends. Think of it as a substitution. By analogy, I like the diet advice that says replace the bagel with fresh almonds and walnuts. Both taste good, and both can fill you up. A diet that only says "stop eating bagels" just make me feel bad. In a similar way, you can choose to spend your after hours time with people instead of with your work computer.

In my experience, as I focused more on the people in my life, I found that my urge to purchase things naturally declined. It is a transition, and it didn't happen by itself. But as I focused on people, they focused more on me. It became a virtuous cycle that felt great.

Does the thought that you may not want to work all the time scare you? If so, it is a sign that your personal identity is too wrapped up in your company. Here is an exercise to help you find substitutes.

What Do You Want Your Legacy to Be?

When you are eighty-five and on your deathbed, who do you want to be there with you? The answer to that question can impact the choices you make today. Think of it as a project plan—envision the end and plan backwards. Are the people you want to be there the people you spend time with now?

Have you ever watched or read Arthur Miller's *Death of a Salesman*?

The play depicts Willie Loman's struggle to suppress a lifetime of regrets by clinging to his illusions. The vision of a salesman's funeral is what keeps him going, a funeral attended by a lifetime of customers and buyers who weep at his passing. Willie wants to be important and liked, and he's sacrificed everything in pursuit of the relationship with his buyers. He sees himself as integral to his company's success, but is fired from his job.

Willie Loman loved to use his hands, but eschewed that path for his life. His house was paid for, his friend offered him an easy job, and yet he chose suicide. And at his funeral, not a single buyer was in attendance, only his family.

I've met people like Willie, who are so consumed by their illusions of greatness that they rationalize their unhappiness, and let life slip by. It doesn't have to be that way.

Getting a Signal

I love the movie *The Matrix*. Neo is offered a chance to get answers to the question that has haunted him his whole life. And from these answers he discovered that his entire life had been a lie, an elaborate illusion constructed by a malevolent computer network.

While nothing so dramatic has occurred in my life, I did get a signal that opened my eyes to my life of corporate idolatry. I told this story back in Chapter 1. I was sitting alone with my thoughts on Yom Kippur, and I was just about to dismiss the sin of idolatry from my mind when I remembered the phrase "You need to do what is best for the company." This led to a flurry of thoughts, which led me to the realization that I had made my company into an idol.

It was a small quiet thought, but I listened and it changed my life. A spiritual teacher once told me that I was smart to listen, because he ignored the signals he was given, and his life had to fall apart before he started to make changes.

My father once told me that he knew alcoholics who suddenly stopped drinking because they "heard something."

"What do you mean?" I asked.

"They heard angel wings," he answered. "The wings of the angel of death. They knew that if they didn't stop drinking, they were going to die."

Is that the answer, to wait until a crisis occurs to make a change? For some people it is. I've shared the stories of Sue and David, who both ignored the signals they were getting and ended up with major health issues.

At a writing conference, I asked a panel how to better market this book. One person came up to me and suggested that I try to reach people who have hit rock bottom. The woman was a psychologist who worked crazy hours until her father got sick, and her life went on tilt trying to deal with it all. She told me she would have ignored my advice until she hit bottom because she was too caught up in her hectic lifestyle.

Another woman at the conference handed me a note that said, "I just buried my fifty-two year old husband due to *Karoshi*, a Japanese word that means death by overwork. He was a brilliant genius." She told me her husband was a workaholic, driven by "inner demons" and couldn't be reached. I still carry that note in my wallet. And a friend of mine had a coworker drop dead of a heart attack at his desk after he was laid off. He had a heart condition, and being laid off was his greatest fear. The layoff was handled in a very insensitive way, and he died cleaning out his cube.

I refuse to believe that nothing can be done until it is too late. I am the proof. I am convinced that I would have had health issues had I continued my ninety-hour workweeks. I am thankful that I listened to that little voice that helped me understand that things could be different.

Listen for the voice. It isn't the voice of fear. It is the voice of hope.

How You Can Kick the Habit of Overwork

Corporate idolatry brings a habit of overwork, and in many ways it is an addiction. In fact, the body can become addicted to the constant adrenaline high of a hectic pace. An adrenaline junkie is someone who is always looking for another thrill. While the term is often associated with extreme sports, it can also be applied to lifestyle prevalent in many aggressive companies. An adrenaline junkie will seek to fill every moment with something, and if things start to slow down, they will take on new assignments. I think I was one, because after I left the corporate world I spent two weeks checking Hotmail every fifteen minutes. It got so ridiculous that I was happy when new junk mail arrived. Then when I could finally settle down and relax, I did nothing more than play Mafia Wars on Facebook.

Work can feel really good, which makes this issue complex. For example, one of the things all of us enjoy is flow—a state of immersion and enjoyment doing a task—and the best parts of a job involve flow. But too much of a good thing always becomes a bad thing. Healthy aspects of work, like company loyalty or work satisfaction, turn into idolatry when the company becomes the most important thing in your life, and it can turn into a full-blown addiction when no sources of flow exist outside the workplace.

So how to kick the habit?

Like losing weight, it's better to take a slow and steady pace as you recover your time. It took me a year to go from ninety to less than sixty hours a week. The more extreme your overwork, the faster you'll start to see the benefits. It's a tipping point kind of thing—retaking the hours at the extremes will help you feel better right away. As I started to recover my time, the first positive result was more and better sleep. I didn't realize how tired I was all the time until I became rested. Being rested always feels better than being sleep deprived.

If you are in a less extreme place, it is important to have one to two hours without work of any kind before bedtime to allow yourself to unwind. This made a huge difference in my life because it opened more time to spend with my wife after the kids went to bed. And it gave me more time to read and watch some TV shows I really liked. I was happier.

Increasing the time every day for rest and renewal will make you feel better, AND it will make you more effective at work.

Expect Nothing from the Employer

One of the secrets to the balanced life is not to expect anything from your employer. Here is what someone wrote a few days after a layoff on an anonymous biotech message board.

"I must admit, it was shocking to me that I was laid off. [The company] gutted the expression business and I was a critical part of the company. I was a key person who [the company] treated like dirt. I hate [the company] for what they did to me, and I hope [specific executives] rot in hell."[112]

It does no good to blame the company. It isn't alive and it isn't capable of having morals. We need to take responsibility for our excess devotion. A person who understood corporate idolatry would never write such a thing. Being sad and feeling a sense of loss are normal, but when it turns into hatred, something is out of balance. I suspect in this case hatred is a reaction against former feelings of love. As the old saying goes, the opposite of love is not hate, but indifference. A healthy dose of indifference can counterbalance feelings of excess devotion.

Why It Is Hard to Say No to the Boss

Putting people first is easy to say, but harder to do when the boss asks you to do something that prioritizes the company over people. While saying no to the boss can be hard, doing so is one of the most important career skills you can learn. In this section, I'll share the secret of saying no to the boss. But first, let's review why we often say yes, even if we don't want to.

Humans have a psychological predisposition to say yes to authority figures. Stanley Milgram, a social psychologist at Yale in the '60s, showed that ordinary people will give painful electronic shocks to strangers if instructed by an authority figure. Participants thought they were testing memory, and started giving shocks of increasing severity when an incorrect answer was given. The recipient (really an actor) behind a partition began to cry out in pain and beg for the experiment to end.

How did people react? Participants got upset, asked to quit, but a man in a white coat told them "the experiment requires you to continue." The shock was given again and again, even when the recipient started groaning and no longer spoke.[113]

So if random people will hurt other people because a stranger in a white coat told them to do so, how much stronger is the compulsion to obey when it is your boss asking you to do something less dastardly? After all, it only means working late. What harm is there? My family will understand. Or one from my past—we don't know for sure that customers won't like the product if we launch it now, and we know for sure that investors will be unhappy if we don't. These rationalizations and illusions keep us in a life of blind obedience.

Living a people-first life provides an escape from the compulsion to obey. In the next section, I will describe a method to help escape the obedience trap. As a hint, for every yes to the guy in the white coat telling you to continue, there was a no to the guy being shocked, who was begging you to stop. One key difference was the white coat, the symbol of authority.

Say Yes to Someone More Important

It is especially hard to say no to the boss—after all, it is part of your job to work on what they tell you to work on. And if you like your boss and the company, saying no is even harder.

But a yes to the boss means a no to someone else. No to a boyfriend. No to the kids. No to the softball team. No to your own need for rest and recharging. No to a healthy dinner. No to a customer who wants a problem solved. Why do all of these things get a no, when your boss gets a yes?

It comes down to values and priorities. The trick to saying no is to remember that work is no higher than the third priority in your life. If you are a believer, I don't need to tell you that God is more important than work. And if you aren't a believer, your health and the people in your life are more important than work.

So when your boss asks you to do something that you want to say no to, think of someone more important in your life, such as a spouse, a child, a friend, or goodness forbid, think of your own needs. If you say yes to the boss and work longer hours, it will take away from one of these more important people in your life. We obey authority figures, so give that other person in your life more authority than your boss.

Imagine this other person is inviting you to be with them. Maybe it is a hike, maybe it is having dinner, maybe it is just sitting together. Imagine them wearing a uniform that says, "NUMBER ONE PRIORITY." Visualize how they look at you. They see you for the person you really are, and love you for it. And because they are more important to you than the company, your mind is clear. You are in the moment with them, free from the mental chatter of the work world.

Say yes to the other person, and then let your boss down easy.

Is a Day Without Work Too Much to Ask?

Now that you are saying no to your boss, I suggest that you work towards having at least one day a week with no work. No slides, no reading, no checking email, no phone calls. I know, there is a perception that we are all expected to be on call all the time. Sometimes this is reality, but more often it is merely perception.

When I was interviewing the seven-day workers, I tried to understand why each person was working every day. Some people said, "Don't blame the company, I'm choosing to do this." I would smile and nod, but I wanted to scream, "Yes, that proves my point! You are choosing to work all the time!"

The other common answer went something like this: "The more senior you are, the more there is an expectation that you need to be available twenty-four seven." Again I nodded, but inside I was thinking of the CEOs and senior VPs I interviewed who said that they felt a day away from work was critical to their success. And I think of the mountain of research showing that rest is critical for high performance.

I think the Jews invented the day off, something we refer to as the Sabbath. Did you know that some Rabbis argue that the Sabbath is the most important holiday in Judaism? Yes, we are commanded to take a holiday every week.

Growing up, I only heard about the strict rules that Orthodox Jews still follow today, like no driving and no turning on the lights. Jewish laws and customs also describe the Sabbath as a taste of the World to Come (Heaven). Shabbat is a day of contemplation and life-affirming activities. For example, Jews are commanded to have a festive meal, take a nap, take a walk in nature, and have sexual intercourse.

While the details are different, Christianity and Islam also have a Sabbath day of rest. Every year the organization Reboot organizes a National Day Of Unplugging, where participants leave the email and Internet behind for a day.[114] Many find it incredibly liberating. Imagine yourself spending the day hanging out with your favorite people, be they friends or family. There is no guilt about not working, no anxiety about checking email. And none of the people you are with are pulling out their phones either. Their attention is on you.

This is something that you can have every week.

The idol-worshipping cultures of the ancient world, like Rome and Greece, criticized the Sabbath because leisure was something for the upper classes only, not to be shared with common workers. In an ironic twist, the corporate idolators of today think that the more senior employees are expected to work more than junior employees. As a consequence, the junior employees want to prove their worth by working all the time.

We can take a lesson from the Sabbath--hard and fast rules to limit work. Maybe the rule for you says that no matter what, the entire family is home to have dinner together on your Sabbath day. Or maybe the rule is that you do not check email one day a week, and you instead spend that day going to the farmers market, playing in an adult sports league, and taking a nap. The rules to limit work should be paired with something you can say yes to. And make it something fun. Run your errands another day.

For me, a day without work means no email, no writing, and no social media. I'll be honest, even today it is hard for me to stick to that schedule. I try, and many weeks I succeed. Living in the post-idolatry world does not mean never making a mistake, or having a problem-free life, but it does mean a deliberate effort to live a balanced life.

How to Think Less about Work and More about Life

The first time I presented the outline for *Busting Your Corporate Idol*, the writing class was split. Some people thought it was an amazing idea that spoke to them. Others were viscerally upset, arguing that the book attacked the basic work ethic and was anti-corporation. It took me only ten minutes to present the outline; we discussed the idea for forty-five minutes.

That class was a safe place to talk. I hope you can find a safe place to re-examine who you are and what is most important to you. An outside perspective can really help. If you play your cards right, you can get your company to pay for an executive coach for "professional development." Once you are behind closed doors, you can ask the coach to help get your life back in balance. Coaches tell me this is very common. A professional therapist can help too.

Maybe you want to change, but are afraid to start. The first step is the hardest, so let me give you some help. Say to yourself out loud, "My company will no longer be my idol. I'm going to start putting people first." Then, begin each day thinking or saying, "I am the kind of person who puts people first." And before you go to bed, take a minute or two to think about the times you put people first. You'll start to see the world differently, and you will begin making different decisions.

This may seem hokey, but if you really want to change, what do you have to lose? Does it seem scary to pull back from work? That is understandable too. You may also feel like you are the only one who has doubts about the corporate life. Believe me, you are not alone.

There is a secret army of people who are starting to speak out and starting to make changes.

The Era of Work Over People Is Coming to an End

I'm incredibly optimistic that the era of busting corporate idols is upon us. Look to the millennial generation—they grew up watching their parents work all the time and want something better for themselves.

More and more, those of us in middle or the end of our careers want a better life too. Even senior executives are starting to publicly admit that it doesn't have to be this way. Ten years ago, it would have been unthinkable that an executive from Goldman Sachs would condemn the company's values in a public resignation letter. But that is exactly what Greg Smith did in March 2012.[115]

In 2007, before the financial meltdown that started the Great Recession, it would have been unthinkable that Erin Callan, then CFO of Lehman Brothers, would one day write about the regret she feels for putting the company first. Yet that is exactly what she wrote in March 2013.[116] Callen wrote:

"I didn't have to be on my BlackBerry from my first moment in the morning to my last moment at night. I didn't have to eat the majority of my meals at my desk. I didn't have to fly overnight to a meeting in Europe on my birthday. I now believe that I could have made it to a similar place [CFO] with at least some better version of a personal life. Not without sacrifice—I don't think I could have 'had it all'—but with somewhat more harmony."

None of us can have it all, but we all can have people who love us. It's just a matter of values and priorities.

Wherever you are in your life, whatever you have done in the past, it is never too late to shift your focus, to bust your corporate idol, and to start putting people first.

The people are there, waiting for you with open arms.

Chapter 10 Questions & Tips

1. What do you want your legacy to be?
2. The most important thing to do is to start.
3. The second most important thing is to remember that everything doesn't need to change overnight. In fact it can't. What is one incremental step that you can make right away?

Notes

1   I am almost as annoyed at people who say that science disproves religion as I am with people who say that religion invalidates evolution. Science explains the way the world works, but it is silent on the most important question, what we should do with that knowledge.

2   Scarboro Missions "Interfaith Commentaries on the Golden Rule" http://www.scarboromissions.ca/Golden_rule/interfaith_commentaries.php

3   Paul Bloom "The Moral Life of Babies" *New York Times* May 5, 2010 http://www.nytimes.com/2010/05/09/magazine/09babies-t.html?pagewanted=all&_r=0

4   J. Kiley Hamlin, Karen Wynn, & Paul Bloom "Social Evaluation By Preverbal Infants." *Nature.* 450 (November 22, 2007): 557-559, doi:10.1038/nature06288

5   Ian K. Smith *Happy: Simple Steps For Getting the Life You Want* (St. Martin's Press, 2010), 190

6   Martha Stout *The Sociopath Next Door* (Three Rivers Press, 2006)

7   Paul Babiak, Craig S. Neumann, and Robert D. Hare "Corporate psychopathy: Talking the Walk." *Behav Sci Law.* (April 6, 2010): 28(2),174-93, doi: 10.1002/bsl.925.

8   Hal Bernton "Dalai Lama urges students to shape the world." *Seattle Times* (15 May 2001). http://archives.seattletimes.nwsource.com/cgi-bin/texis.cgi/web/vortex/display?slug=dalai15m0&date=20010515 Retrieved 29 Feb 2012.

9   http://www.katinkahesselink.net/sufi/quotes.html retrieved 3/21/2012

10 http://www.quotationspage.com/quote/2534.html

11 Freeh, Sporkin & Sullivan, LLP *Report of the Special Investigative Counsel Regarding the Actions of The Pennsylvania State University Related to the Child Sexual Abuse Committed by Gerald A. Sandusky* (July 12, 2012) http://progress.psu.edu/assets/content/REPORT_FINAL_071212.pdf

12 Melissa Dribben "TVs At PSU Student Center Suddenly Switched To Public Access" *Philly.com* (July 13, 2012) retrieved June 10, 2013. http://articles.philly.com/2012-07-13/news/32649437_1_student-center-public-access-freeh-report

13 I combined two photos by Michael Bentley that I found on Flickr available under a creative commons license. You can see the originals here.www.flickr.com/photos/donhomer/2131200670/ and here www.flickr.com/photos/donhomer/2131201034/ I uploaded the combined photo here http://www.flickr.com/photos/72592973@N03/7584364906/

14 Jason Whitlock "Sexism Played Role In Penn St. Horror" *Foxsports.com* (July 14, 2012) retrieved July 16, 2012 http://msn.foxsports.com/collegefootball/story/all-male-hierarchy-sexism-played-role-in-penn-state-joe-paterno-jerry-sandusky-cover-up-071212

15 Jessica Bennett and Jacob Bernstein "Meet Penn State's New Whistleblower, Vicky Triponey" *The Daily Beast* (Nov 23, 2011, Retrieved July 15, 2012) http://www.thedailybeast.com/articles/2011/11/23/meet-penn-state-s-new-whistleblower-vicky-triponey.html

16 Freeh p 14

17 Freeh p 75

18 Freeh p 65

19 Bryan W. Husted and David Bruce Allen *Corporate Social Strategy: Stakeholder Engagement and Competitive Advantage* (Cambridge University Press 2010), 141-142. Google eBook.

20 *Dartmouth College v. Woodward*, http://en.wikipedia.org/wiki/Corporation Retrieved July 29, 2012

21 Carlton Wynne "Is Idolatry the New Sin?" *Reformation 21.org* November 2009. http://www.reformation21.org/articles/is-idolatry-the-new-sin.php

22 The Child Labor Education Project "Child Labor in US History" Last updated July 2011. Retrieved August 2012 http://www.continuetolearn.uiowa.edu/laborctr/child_labor/about/us_history.html

23 Juliet Macur "Americans Excel, but Wieber Is Out for All-Around" *nytimes.com* July 29, 2012 http://tinyurl.com/lgdx4ao

24 The other three woman were Anastasia Grishina (RUS, 12th place); Jennifer Pinches (GBR, 21st place); and Yao Jinnan (CHN, 22nd place).

25 MaryFran Bontempo "Sex--The Other Olympic Sport" *Technorati.com* July 28, 2012 Retrieved August 15, 2013 http://technorati.com/women/article/sex-the-other-olympic-sport/

26 Alain De Botton *The Pleasures and Sorrows of Work*. (New York: Pantheon, 2009), 80

27   De Botton p82

28   Transcription of the 2005 Kenyon Commencement Address - May 21, 2005 retrieved August 5, 2012. http://web.archive.org/web/20080213082423/ http://www.marginalia.org/dfw_kenyon_commencement.html;

29   Dictionary.com

30   Thomas J Peters and Robert H. Waterman Jr. *In Search Of Excellence: Lessons From America's Best-Run Companies.* (Harper and Row 1982, 282.

31   Peters p. 51.

32   Peters p. 76.

33   Frederick Reichheld *The Loyalty Effect: the Hidden Force Behind Growth, Profits, and Lasting Value* (Harvard Business School Press 1996), 127-.

34   Reichheld p. 111

35   Reichheld p. 306

36   Reichheld p. 153

37   Reichheld p. 156

38   Patrick Thibodeau "HP to cut salaries as profits decline; CEO takes hit, too. Hurd to take 20% pay cut as Hewlett-Packard looks to lower costs after weak Q1" *Computerworld.com* February 19, 2009. Retrieved August 14, 2012.

39   Questions and Answers about OVERWORK: A Sloan Work and Family Research Network Fact Sheet. (Last Updated May 2009). https://workfamily.sas.upenn.edu/sites/workfamily.sas.upenn.edu/files/imported/pdfs/overwork.pdf

40   Tzvi Freeman "What's So Terrible About Idolatry?" *Chabbad.org* Retrieved April 12, 2013 http://www.chabad.org/library/article_cdo/aid/3201/jewish/Whats-So-Terrible-About-Idolatry.htm

41   Peters p 77-78

42   Linda Treviño is Distinguished Professor of Organizational Behavior and Ethics, and Director of the Shoemaker Program in Business Ethics in the Smeal College of Business at Penn State University. She is the author of over 70 articles as well as several books.

43 Jennifer J Kish-Gephart, David A Harrison, Linda Klebe Treviño, "Bad apples, bad cases, and bad barrels: Meta-analytic evidence about sources of unethical decisions at work." *Journal of Applied Psychology* Vol 95 no1 (Jan 2010) 1-31. doi: 10.1037/a0017103

44 Kish-Gephart P. 20

45 Kish-Gephart P. 21

46 Ibid

47 Ibid

48 Craig D. Parks and Asako B. Stone "The Desire to Expel Unselfish Members From the Group" *Journal of Personality and Social Psychology* Volume 99, Issue 2, (August 2010), 303-310

49 Quote from Paul Nunes, executive director of research at the Accenture Institute for High Performance, commenting on the article Your Most Helpful Colleague (Don't You Hate Him?) by Craig Parks http://blogs.hbr.org/cs/2010/09/when_selfless_behavior_in_a_gr.html cited October 25, 2011

50 Timothy Judge, Beth Livingston and Charlice Hurst. "Do Nice Guys and Gals Really Finish Last? The Joint Effects of Sex and Agreeableness on Income" *Journal of Personal and Social Psychology* Vol 102 no 2 (Feb 2012), 390-407. doi: 10.1037/a0026021
Note: agreeableness is a term in social psychology that refers to "trust, straightforwardness, altruism, compliance, modesty, and tender-mindedness."

51 John Malkovich refers to this fable at the end of the movie Dangerous Liaisons as he betrays the love of his life. For more, see what Wikipedia has to say. http://en.wikipedia.org/wiki/The_Scorpion_and_the_Frog

52 Walter Isaacson *Steve Jobs* (Simon & Schuster 2011), 117-120.

53 http://www.aesops-fables.org.uk/aesop-fable-the-fox-and-the-crow.htm

54 Hayyim Nahman Bialik, Yehoshua Ḥana Rawnitzki, eds., and William G. Braude trans. *The Book of Legends/Sefer Ha-aggadah : Legends from the Talmud and Midrash.* (New York: Schocken, 1992), 245:194

55 Wikipedia contributors, "Illusion of control" Wikipedia, The Free Encyclopedia, retrieved September 20, 2012 http://en.wikipedia.org/wiki/Illusion_of_control

56 Mark Fenton-O'Creevy,; Nigel Nicholson, Emma Soane, and Paul Willman "Trading on illusions: Unrealistic perceptions of control and trading performance," *Journal of Occupational and Organizational Psychology* (British Psychological Society, 2003), **76**: 53–68 Via Wikipedia http://en.wikipedia.org/wiki/Illusion_of_control

57 Suzanne C Thompson "Illusions of control," in *Cognitive Illusions: A Handbook on Fallacies and Biases in Thinking, Judgment and Memory*, ed Rüdiger Pohl, (Psychology Press 2004), pp. 122 Via Wikipedia http://bit.ly/18bhFax

58 Inspired by a story from the Talmud. Tractate Berachos, 32a,

59 Christopher Chabris and Daniel Simons *The Invisible Gorilla And Other Ways Our Intuitions Deceive Us* (Crown 2010), 55-57.

60 Chabris p 57

61 American Management Association "The Ethical Enterprise: A Global Study of Business Ethics 2005-2015" (2005). http://www.amanet.org/HR-EthicsSurvey06.pdf P 5

62 Ibid

63 http://dictionary.cambridge.org/dictionary/business-english/revenue-forecast

64 Maimonides *Mishneh Torah Volume 3: Hilchot Avodat Kochavim*. ed Eliyahu Touger (Moznaim 1990), 212-213

65 Nassim Nicholas Taleb *The Black Swan* (Random House 2007), 148-150.

66 Greg Smith "Why I Am Leaving Goldman Sachs" *NY Times Opinionator* Published: March 14, 2012. Retrieved June 16, 2013. http://www.nytimes.com/2012/03/14/opinion/why-i-am-leaving-goldman-sachs.html?pagewanted=all&_r=0

67 Reichheld p. 302-5.

68 Rollin Bishop "Yahoo! Slowly Becoming Google, Finally Offers Free Lunch" *Geek system (blog)* July 30th 2012 http://www.geekosystem.com/yahoo-free-lunch/

69 Vasanth Sridharan "Google's Ginormous Free Food Budget: $7,530 Per Googler, $72 Million A Year*" *Business Insider* Apr. 23, 2008 retrieved October 24, 2012 http://read.bi/16mg9R8

70 "Google's 'free food' is not free" *Rachelbythebay.com (blog)* Saturday, January 21, 2012 Retrieved April 15, 2013 http://rachelbythebay.com/w/2012/01/21/notfree/

71 Jonathan Strickland "How the Googleplex Works" *howstuffworks.com* retrieved October 24, 2012 http://computer.howstuffworks.com/googleplex3.htm

72 Kish-Gephart p 21

73 ibid

74 James G. March *Primer on Decision Making: How Decisions Happen* (Free Press. 1994), 64-65

75 Matthew 6:21 http://bible.cc/matthew/6-21.htm

76 Charles Duhigg *The Power of Habit. Why We Do What We Do In Life and Business* (Random House 2012), 19

77 Duhigg p 49-51

78 Duhigg 275-86

79 Chip Heath and Dan Heath *Switch: How To Change Things When Change is Hard* (Broadway Books, 2010) p 114.

80 American Psychological Association Practice Organization. (2010). Psychologically Healthy Workplace Program Fact Sheet: By the Numbers. http://www.phwa.org/dl/2010phwp_fact_sheet.pdf

81 http://www.cdc.gov/features/dssleep/

82 American Psychological Association Practice Organization. (2010). *Psychologically Healthy Workplace Program Fact Sheet: By the Numbers.* Retrieved from http://www.phwa.org/dl/2010phwp_fact_sheet.pdf

83 Jonathan Haidt. *The Happiness Hypothesis* Online PDF p. 4 http://www.happinesshypothesis.com/ http://www.happinesshypothesis.com/happiness-hypothesis-ch1.pdf retrieved November 12, 2012 from http://www.happinesshypothesis.com/chapters.html

84 Mayer accepted the CEO position at Yahoo while pregnant. While there was a great outcry from both sides of the mommy wars about a pregnant CEO, from a business standpoint this was a non-event.

85 Rabbi Marder was quoting "Chaim David HaLevy, former Sephardic Chief Rabbi of Israel from [Aseh L'cha Rav, 2:64; quoted in Work, Workers and the Jewish Owner].

86 Rabbi Marder's entire sermon available here

87 Robert Putnam *Bowling Alone: The Collapse and Revival of American Community* Touchtone Books (2001)

88 Social Capital blog http://socialcapital.wordpress.com/2010/10/27/summary-of-recent-happiness-research/

89 Ian Smith p 190

90 *Create Rituals to Get More Done* Harvard Business Review Management Tip December 19, 2012 Retrieved April 16, 2013 Adapted from Trapani et. al. Guide to Getting the Right Work Done HBR Press http://hbr.org/tip?date=121912&utm_campaign=Socialflow&utm_source=Socialflow&utm_medium=Tweet

91 Laszlo Bock "Passion, Not Perks" *Google Think Insights* (September, 2011) http://www.google.com/think/articles/passion-not-perks.html

92 R Ulrich "View through a window may influence recovery from surgery." *Science* (Apr 27; 1984) Vol 224, 420-1.

93 "Green environments essential for human health" *Phys.org* April 19, 2011 retrieved December 23, 2012 http://phys.org/news/2011-04-green-environments-essential-human-health.html

94 Michael Bernstein "In the green of health: Just 5 minutes of 'green exercise' optimal for good mental health" *Phys.org* May 21, 2011. Retrieved December 23, 2012 http://bit.ly/16fc67Y

95 *Marian Cook* "Leadership Skills: Organizational Savvy (Part 1 of 3)" *WITI.com* http://www.witi.com/wire/articles/96/Leadership-Skills:-Organizational-Savvy-(Part-1-of-3)/ *Retrieved January 7, 2013.*

96 Viktor E. Frankl *Man's Search For Meaning* (Beacon Press, 2006)

97 Antony Page and Robert A. Katz "Freezing Out Ben & Jerry: Corporate Law and the Sale Of a Social Enterprise Icon" *Stanford Social Innovation Review* (Fall 2012), retrieved January 21, 2013 http://www.ssireview.org/articles/entry/the_truth_about_ben_and_jerrys

98   Hilary Howard "Socially Conscious Companies Have a New Yardstick" *New York Times*. Published: November 8, 2012, retrieved January 21, 2013. http://www.nytimes.com/2012/11/09/giving/a-new-yardstick-for-socially-conscious-companies.html?pagewanted=all&_r=0

99   Kish-Gephart p21

100 Daniel H. Pink *Drive: The Surprising Truth about What Motivates Us*. (New York, NY: Riverhead, 2009),84-85.

101 Results Only Work Environment Case Study: GAP http://www.gorowe.com/blog/2013/01/06/rowe-stories/case-study-how-a-retail-giant-made-big-changes-to-workplace-culture/

102 Ibid

103 Results Only Work Environment Case Study: Suntell http://info.gorowe.com/case-study-software-company-demonstrates-success-with-rowe/

104 Jody Thompson speaking at Telework Summit 2012. http://www.youtube.com/watch?v=_DhIVfpfimY&noredirect=1 retrieved August 20, 2013.

105 Center For Disease Control "Insufficient Sleep Is a Public Health Epidemic" http://1.usa.gov/16mgvXJ Retrieved April 21, 2013. The web page sites the publication below for the 30% statistic. Schoenborn CA, Adams PF. Health behaviors of adults: United States, 2005–2007. National Center for Health Statistics. *Vital Health Stat* 10(245). 2010.

106 James Maas Sleep For Success Webpage http://www.powersleep.org/ retrieved August 20, 2013

107 Lauren Weber "Go Ahead, Hit the Snooze Button" *Wall Street Journal Online* Updated January 23, 2013, Retrieved April 21, 2013. http://online.wsj.com/article/SB10001424127887323301104578257894191502654.html

108 Pamela Stone "Bravo to Sheryl Sandberg for leaving work". *CNN.com* updated Tue April 17, 2012. Retrieved June 19, 2013. http://www.cnn.com/2012/04/16/opinion/stone-leave-work-day/index.html

109 Linda Hill and Kent Lineback "Stop Avoiding Office Politics" November 2, 2011. *HBR Blog Network* Retrieved April 21, 2013 http://blogs.hbr.org/hill-lineback/2011/11/stop-avoiding-office-politics.html

110 Ibid

111 Ibid

112 Anonymous submitter *Biotech Rumor Mill* http://www.biofind.com/rumor-mill/affymetrix-layoffs-company-burning-death Submitted on February 7, 2013 Retrieved April 21, 2013

113 Watch the video footage of the actual experiment, it's shocking! http://www.youtube.com/watch?v=yr5cjyokVUs&feature=player_embedded

114 http://nationaldayofunplugging.com/

115 Greg Smith

116 Is There Life After Work? by Erin Callan New York Times: March 9, 2013. http://www.nytimes.com/2013/03/10/opinion/sunday/is-there-life-after-work.html?_r=2& Retrieved April 25, 2013

Acknowledgements

This book has been a four year project, and I couldn't have done it without the help and support from an army of people.

My wife Rachel Kindt, without whom none of this would be possible, and for my daughters who have made my time at home such a joy.

To everyone who shared their story for me. It takes courage to tell your story, even if anonymously. You've given hope to thousands of people who feel like they are alone with their chronic overwork.

My editors Laura Carlson & Hillel Black, and to my cover designer Ranilo Cabo.

Nina Amir, for writing How To Blog a Book, which helped me break through and get the book done. And thanks for introducing me to Hillel.

Tijen Sumbul for teaching me about Ethnography and interviewing, and Casey FitzSimons for early feedback on the book outline.

My readers who gave me great feedback and encouragement on the book in its various stages:

David Marchetti

David Hanna
Rick Rosenthal
Stephanie Martinson
Rachel Tasch
Robert Badame
Alan Warshaw
Alan Dance
Jarie Bolander
Audry Long
Janet Marder
Sarah Weissman
Jennifer Clayman

My Tuesday writing group at the mechanics institute who have given me such wonderful feedback over the years, and didn't throw me out at first for having a crazy idea poorly written.

Janet Holland
Eric Meub
Terry Ryan
Adele Fasick
Daniel Hill
Clae Styron
Kathy Gilbert
Priscilla Burgess
Mark Maginn

My original writing partners: Diane Olberg & Dick Ferrington. Thanks for putting up with me rewriting the same outline and chapter over and over again. Your encouragement kept me going through the first year of the project. And thank you to Steve Albert who taught the writing class where we met. Steve, your comment on my original outline was "on track." It kept me going.

To all my amigos in the Dragonwriters Facebook group – you are too many to name.

To Len Fonte, my 12th grade English teacher who told me at graduation that he couldn't believe that I was going to study science in college. Thank you. I never forgot it, and I guess you were on to something.

To Mike Spanton & Joe Milligan, for saying hi to me at the coffee shop every day, and to all baristas within a ten mile radius of San Carlos, CA.

The thousands of you who have visited the Idolbuster. Your numbers and secret feedback told me that I was onto something.

To my parents David Marcus and Elaine Marcus for all your love and support over the years.

About the Author

*I*n 2005, Greg Marcus was working 90 hours a week as a marketer in the biotech industry. On Yom Kippur, the Jewish Day of Atonement, Greg started thinking about the sin of idolatry. Just as he was about to dismiss idolatry as something no longer relevant in the modern world, he remembered the phrase "you need to do what is best for the company." Greg realized that he was not the family-first person he though he was, and that he had made an idol out of his company. &at realization changed his life—a year later he was working less than sixty hours a week without changing jobs. The secret? He decided to put people first.

Greg has a B.A. from Cornell University, and a Ph.D. from MIT. Through his writing, speaking, and coaching, Dr. Greg helps the chronically overworked find life balance. He lives in the San Francisco Bay Area.

If you are looking for more balance in your life, please visit Greg's website Idolbuster.com to schedule a free strategy session.

www.ingramcontent.com/pod-product-compliance
Lightning Source LLC
LaVergne TN
LVHW051049080426
835508LV00019B/1784